Gender and the

Praise for this book

'Much of the commentary on the 2007/8 crisis has focused on the financial sector, its epicentre, or at best, on its implications for the "real economy" in terms of economic slowdown and unemployment in the North. Much less attention has been given to developing countries which have been embroiled in these crises even if they did not play a part in creating them. What this timely volume documents through its empirically grounded case studies and analytical contributions, is a gendered analysis of the 2007/8 crisis seen through the interrelated spheres of finance, production and reproduction, which demystifies it by showing its full effects on the lives of real women and men in developing countries. Equally refreshing is the long-term perspective of the volume: rather than presenting the crisis as a sudden and abrupt event, what it shows is that it was the culmination of more than three decades of 'Washington Consensus' policies of liberalization and commercialization (often through debt-related conditionalities). These policies increased income inequalities, overstretched women's time and energies as workers and carers, and exposed families and households to systemic risks, without putting in place the social security systems that could increase resilience and recovery.'

Shahra Razavi, Research Coordinator,
United Nations Research Institute for Social Development

'This is to my knowledge the first book on the gender impacts of the current financial crisis and the global recession following the crisis. It is an enormous accomplishment to have brought together such a diverse collection of up-to-date papers with surprisingly recent data. The major strength of this collection of papers lies in its diversity, both regional as well as thematic. In addition, it contains a thorough analytical framework for evaluating the crisis and recession from a gender perspective, by Diane Elson. Together, this book provides a unique, early insight into the gendered effects of the crisis well before national level gender disaggregated data have come available through official statistics. It thereby leaves no excuse to policy makers to ignore possible negative gender effects of their policies.'

Irene van Staveren, Professor of Pluralist Development Economics,
Institute of Social Studies of Erasmus University Rotterdam

Gender and the
Economic Crisis

Edited by Ruth Pearson and Caroline Sweetman

Published by Practical Action Publishing in association with Oxfam GB

Practical Action Publishing Ltd
Schumacher Centre for Technology and Development
Bourton on Dunsmore, Rugby,
Warwickshire, CV23 9QZ, UK
www.practicalactionpublishing.org

Since 1974, Practical Action Publishing (formerly Intermediate Technology
Publications and ITDG Publishing) has published and disseminated books and
information in support of international development work throughout the world.
Practical Action Publishing is a trading name of Practical Action Publishing Ltd
(Company Reg. No. 1159018), the wholly owned publishing company of Practical
Action. Practical Action Publishing trades only in support of its parent charity objec-
tives and any profits are covenanted back to Practical Action (Charity Reg. No. 247257,
Group VAT Registration No. 880 9924 76).

Oxfam is a registered charity in England and Wales (no 202918) and Scotland (SC
039042). Oxfam GB is a member of Oxfam International.

Oxfam GB,
Oxfam House, John Smith Drive,
Oxford, OX4 2JY, UK
www.oxfam.org.uk

Cover photo: Workers demonstrate in front of Sama garments in Dhaka against
the laying off of workers without warning for seven days. Dhaka, Bangladesh
(26 May 2007). Credit: Copyright © Munir uz Zaman / DrikNEWS / Majority World
Indexed by Daphne Lawless, Pindar NZ, Auckland, New Zealand
Typeset by Pindar NZ, Auckland, New Zealand
Printed by Hobbs the Printers Ltd
Printed on FSC 100% post-consumer waste recycled paper.

Contents

Figures

Tables

CHAPTER 1
Introduction

Ruth Pearson and Caroline Sweetman

This chapter first appeared in *Gender & Development* 18(2), pp. 165–77, July 2010.

In 2007, a paralysing financial crisis and economic downturn shook the global economy. Three years on, countries in both the industrialized and the developing worlds are facing a number of complex and inter-related economic challenges. The economic crisis is effectively part of a triple crisis, coming on top of a crisis in food and fuel affordability and availability. This triple crisis is threatening the well-being of an estimated 40 million women, men and children in poverty, and also threatens a further 120 million who are currently living just above the poverty line, and who are at risk of falling below it (World Bank, 2010).

This issue of *Gender & Development* forms a part of an innovative learning project to understand the impact of the global economic crisis, which raged from 2007–09, on the lives of poor women, men and children living in developing countries, through the lens of gender analysis. Ultimately, we hope that the case studies and analysis featured in this issue, and in other elements of our learning project, will improve the responses of policymakers in both government and NGOs to the crisis.[1] In particular, policymakers and programme planners in governments and NGOs need to recognize the existence and importance of unpaid economic activity – often care work, mostly performed by women – in underpinning national economies and individual households. All the articles here present the case for national and international economic recovery policies, and the support programmes offered to communities by development workers, to be sensitive to these realities, and in particular to the differences in the interests and needs of women, as compared to men.

Policymakers, practitioners, and the lobbyists and advocates aiming to influence them, need to listen very carefully to poor women and men whose lives are being affected by the current crisis. One clear message is that this latest economic shock comes on top of a range of other development challenges and problems. Whilst it would seem that not all developing countries are affected by this crisis – indeed, major southern economies such as India, China and Uganda seem to have been minimally affected by it – other countries, particularly those with a big export sector and small domestic market have been damaged. Charting the ways in which the economic crisis is worsening pre-existing disadvantage, and deepening poverty, the articles here emphasize that the crisis needs to be understood as the last straw for many women, men and children.

There are millions of people whose options were already exhausted before the crisis, in the face of challenges including climate change, disease – in particular the HIV epidemic, which continues to rage in much of sub-Saharan Africa and beyond – and the food crisis, which saw the prices of basic foodstuffs soar in the mid 2000s, partly because land was being diverted to growing biofuels, threatening the food security of impoverished households, as poor countries were forced to import food. Individuals, households and communities have been brought to breaking point by this latest crisis.

To talk of the 'coping mechanisms' and recognize the resilience of people in poverty is important, but their ability to weather economic and social crises should not be romanticized, or seen in too optimistic a light. In particular, women's contribution to economic survival and recovery, as well as their crucial role in the realization of development goals in the future, needs to be supported.

Mapping and understanding the economic crisis

This crisis differs from previous global and regional economic crises in a number of ways. A health warning is required when looking at the work of many current commentators on the economic crisis: they are mostly relying on *a priori*, theoretical analysis, based on studies of previous crises and dramatic changes to the macroeconomic environment. In particular, they are focusing on the impact of economic Structural Adjustment Programmes (SAPs), in the 1980s (for example, Cornia, Jolly and Stewart 1987 critiqued on this); and the Asian financial crisis of the late 1990s (see Garg et al., 1999, or Weisbrot, 2007, for an analysis of the impact of this crisis).

In contrast, the articles in this issue present detailed case studies which offer a snapshot of what was happening in 2009–10, immediately after the first aftershocks of the 2007–09 crisis were reverberating around the world. They aspire to construct an overview of what was happening, from a gendered economic perspective, yet to remain realistic about the limitations of the analysis possible at this moment.

Unlike earlier crises, the financial crisis of 2007–09 was generated in the global North, so in some respects it can be argued that its impact on the global South was indirect. This contrasts with the global recession of the 1970s–1980s, which followed the oil crisis, and the Asian financial crisis of the late 1990s, both of which directly involved economies in developing countries. The current economic crisis, which began as a collapse of the US sub-prime mortgage market, rapidly spread to other sectors of the US economy, and then to other OECD countries. It led to the collapse of key financial institutions, a shortage of loan finance in the housing and industrial sectors, and a general down-turn in investment and trade in the global economy. After decades of expansion of home ownership in North America and Europe, the startling rates of inflation in housing and property prices, a feature of the past two decades, were reversed. The key global financial institutions in Northern countries effectively suffered a collective loss of confidence in each other, and in the value of the complex financial instruments that they had created, leading to the collapse of major finance companies, such as Lehmann Brothers. The markets then responded by reducing investments, and restricting credit. These changes have been accompanied by increases in unemployment, and reduced consumer spending (Lawson and King, 2008).

As Stephanie Seguino points out in her article in this collection, the main victims of the economic crisis in the global North have been low-income families, where income-earners are either losing their jobs, or find their wages are losing their real value in the face of rising food costs, and escalating interest rates on home loans and other credit agreements. Many of these families are losing their homes and their jobs. Women and ethnic minority workers have been particularly hard hit, not just by job losses, but also by reductions in hours of work, wage rates and non-wage benefits.

In response to the current crisis, various Northern governments and banking authorities have sought to underpin their economies with expansive monetary policies ('quantitative easing'), and fiscal interventions, which aim to increase demand, and stimulate the economy ('fiscal stimulus programmes'). The latter focus on boosting those economic sectors seen as 'key', including the car industry and construction, which employ a mainly male workforce, and had suffered most unemployment as the result of the crisis. These measures have had dramatic effects on the public purse, and governments in the global North, especially in West and Eastern Europe, are currently racing to take measures to cut the budget deficit. The fear is that this will translate into a reduction in spending on social and welfare services, such as health, education, social protection and social security. These are all areas of social provisioning which represent government investment in the well-being and development of current and future generations. The main beneficiaries of such services are the elderly, the sick, parents and children. In economic terms, cutting back on such services represents a reduction in investment in human capital. These measures have a particular impact on women, due to their gendered responsibilities for family care and well-being.

Understanding the impact on countries of the global South

As noted earlier, this economic crisis originated in the global North, and there has been a general assumption on the part of many economists that developing countries have been only indirectly affected, and therefore, that the crisis is less of a problem for them than it is for the economies of the industrialized North. The logic of their arguments is that countries of the global South have financial institutions and systems that are less integrated into the international financial markets.

We stated above that not all economies in the global South have been affected, and there is some evidence that major economies, such as India, have recovered swiftly in terms of levels of economic growth, though often this has been without a corresponding rise in employment. But many of the more exposed economies are finding that their ability to respond to the current economic downturn has been seriously affected by the changes in global economic and financial regulation that they underwent prior to the economic crisis. Decades of liberalization of trade, investment and capital markets, following the 'Washington Consensus',[2] articulated by the international financial institutions (IFIs), have had significant consequences for many developing economies.

First, the SAPs of the 1980s and 1990s promoted export-led economic growth in developing countries, and, in so doing, subordinated the needs of their domestic economies to the needs of the export sectors. Second, currency devaluations and the need to achieve a reasonable balance between the foreign exchange earned by exports and inflows of finance, and that spent on imports and debt servicing, increased the competitiveness of many export-oriented industries. However, it has also caused a decline in real incomes in other sectors, as subsidies and guaranteed prices were withdrawn. Third, SAPs required governments to cut down the size of the state itself, and to adopt policies which introduced cash payments for social services, as well as promoting the role of the private sector, not only in production, but also as a provider of social services. This has led to households having to find money to pay for services, and made it really difficult for poor households to shield themselves from the vagaries of the macroeconomy without any external support.

In her article in this issue, Diane Elson presents a gendered framework for understanding the impact of the 2007–09 crisis, which captures some of the complex ways in which it is affecting developing economies, and the economic and social implications. This framework is useful in enabling us to understand the impact of the crisis on countries of both the global North and South.

Diane Elson argues that it is necessary to distinguish between the *financial* sphere of the economy which, as we have noted above, is where the crisis originated; the *productive* sphere – where goods and services are produced, which is the focus of much commentary in terms of the effect on employment and incomes; and the *reproductive* sphere, which is where human labour and capital are reproduced over different generations. The reproductive sphere includes all work undertaken to care for human beings. In Diane Elson's definition, it includes 'unpaid work in families and communities, organized unpaid volunteer work, and paid (but non-market) work in public services like health and education' (Elson, this volume, Chapter 3). Although the reproductive economy is often excluded from standard analyses of the economy, it is crucial to include it if we are to understand the full effects of the economic crisis on the lives, as well as the livelihoods, of poor women and men in developing countries.

Diane Elson's tripartite distinction between different spheres of the economy is useful in guiding our understanding of the impact of the crisis, particularly on women in the global South. But at present, there is little empirical research, and a lack of longitudinal data on the effects on different sectors of the economy – let alone focused studies of the gender issues playing out – in particular of the fate of women. Serious analysis, that includes the impact on reproduction as well as finance and production, needs to take a long-term perspective, since we are talking about 'growing' new generations of people, and caring for current generations – not just workers, but the sick, elderly, unpaid carers, and so on.

It is not at all clear that the crisis has finished working its way through the world economy; or that, particularly in European economies, there will not be a further (double dip) recession in the months and years to come (Evans-Pritchard, 2010). The impact of the crisis needs to be tracked over time, which will involve collecting and analysing longitudinal data from statistical sources and from qualitative research and observation, such as the community sentinel monitoring proposed by Diane Elson.[3] Only by doing this kind of monitoring can we hope to respond to the unfolding and evolving needs of the women, men and children affected by the crisis, as it plays out in different contexts, over months and years to come.

The financial sector

The effect of the economic crisis on the financial sector in developing countries is already beginning to be observed. Poor women and men need money, to use as working capital for small businesses, but also to purchase food and household essentials, as well as pay for health services and school fees. For the past three decades, women have been targeted by microfinance institutions as their borrowers of choice, due to their relatively high rates of repayment (Johnson and Rogaly, 1997); the fact that women are more likely to spend earnings on family welfare (Bruce, 1989); and notions of empowering women through greater access to material resources (Mayoux, 2002).

The impact of the current crisis on the financial sector in developing countries, in relation to poor women and men, is not easy to chart, since much more research is needed. Microfinance institutions, which are the major source of lending to poor women in the global South, are reporting that people are borrowing more than they can repay, and becoming over-indebted. Would-be entrepreneurs are facing new challenges in their businesses, due to market saturation. This is leading to fears about borrowers' capacity to repay, and, in some cases, to lenders adopting repressive measures to try to frighten people into meeting their obligations (Sobhani and Sivakumaran, 2009). There are worries that cutbacks on microfinance will force poor women – and men – into the hands of informal moneylenders, who charge high rates of interest. Some analysts are already reporting that the desperate need to retain a cash income in times of economic stress is leading to the growth in trafficking of women, in drug- and arms-trading in poor communities, in escalating levels of violence, and in an increase in teenage pregnancies and sexually transmitted diseases, as girls trade sex for cash (Hossain, 2009).

However, these issues are not the focus of policy for the IFIs and Northern governments. Their concern is to restore financial stability. Their strategy is, therefore, to channel huge amounts of public money into securing the sustainability of major banks and other finance companies.

The productive sector

The implications for women of the crisis in the production sector are more tangible, but even here there is no uniform trend. Relatively early in the crisis, researchers began to highlight the impact of the crisis on women's formal employment in developing countries, focusing on skilled and unskilled workers employed in export processing. This type of employment is often precarious in terms of its conditions of employment, failing to guarantee women long-term work (Oxfam, 2004). In many countries, governments have followed a policy of waiving standard employment laws for companies operating in export-processing zones, in order to attract international investors and companies, or alternatively, have turned a blind eye to infringements of labour laws (Barrientos and Smith, 2006).

An assumption that the economic crisis would negatively affect women's formal employment in the global South, in terms of both quantity and quality of employment, was made early on by many individuals and organizations. The logic behind this assumption was that there was clearly a reduction in demand for export goods produced in sectors dominated by a female labour force in the global South. There has indeed been some evidence that this assumption was correct, in some contexts: for example, Thailand (World Bank, 2008). Other researchers report large-scale lay-offs in the garment industry in Cambodia (ILO, 2009).

In her article, Reineira Arguello, of the international NGO Womankind Worldwide, discusses the impact of the economic crisis on women farm-workers in agri-business in Peru. Pre-existing gender inequalities have worsened women's situation in the labour market during the crisis. Households that are solely, or mainly, dependent on women's wages are more likely than others to be poor to start with, and the women in these households have weaker bargaining power with their employers. They are much more likely, therefore, to find their working conditions and pay worsening as a result of the crisis, or to be laid off altogether. Unemployment is plunging many into acute poverty.

A second article in this issue focusing on the impact of the crisis on women production workers draws on Oxfam research with women textile and garment workers in the Calabarzon area of the Philippines. Women make up the majority of the workforce in these largely export-oriented industries. Many crisis-triggered company closures, retrenchments, and lay-offs have been occurring. The study suggests that 'formally employed women in the electronics, semiconductors, telecommunications and garment industries, as well as the other industries engaged in production for export, have been the hardest hit by the crisis' (Gaerlan et al., 2010: 230).

The impact of the crisis on the employment of migrant workers is another key area of enquiry. Migrant work represents a lifeline to many poor families in the global South. Many of the workers employed in labour-intensive industry in the global South are migrants from even poorer countries who offer the cheapest labour, at the least cost to employers, as Jackie Pollock and Soe Lin Aung point out in their article on migrant workers in Thailand. As noted earlier, labour-intensive export sectors are large employers of women; what is less often acknowledged is that these sectors frequently employ migrant workers who rarely receive the minimum wage, or involve employers in any non-wage payments.

Migrant workers are not the only ones to find themselves without protection and regulation, forced to face the recession without any assistance or social safety nets offered by the state. In vast areas of the world, including most of sub-Saharan Africa, the formal sector employs only a very small percentage of adult men, and even fewer women. Many have never experienced formal employment. The majority of the working poor are forced to make their living – in activities and businesses which are often not registered, where there are no employment contracts, which often rely on (unpaid) family labour, and where workers have no access to unemployment benefits, health insurance or sickness pay, or any of the other non-wage benefits associated with formal work. Studies of the impact of the crisis on women workers in the informal economy report rises in hours of work, decreases in wages, increased vulnerability to physical and sexual harassment and a growing perception of powerlessness and vulnerability amongst women workers (Dullnig et al., 2010).

Inevitably, reductions in employment in the formal economy (due to reduced consumer demand for export goods), and escalating food and fuel prices, are forcing more and more people into the informal economy, to try to earn enough to feed, clothe and educate their families. But, as Jennifer Cohen highlights in her article, the informal sector is already overcrowded, and most people in it are barely making enough to live on. She argues that it is impossible in the South African context for the informal economy to absorb the many thousands of additional workers, including people currently retrenched from formal jobs who are seeking to survive by stepping up existing sideline businesses or starting new ones.

Another writer in this issue who focuses on the informal economy and the impact of the economic crisis on workers in this sector is Zoe Horn, who presents findings from an interesting study undertaken by the Inclusive Cities Project and WIEGO. This research was carried out with three important groups of informal sector workers – street traders, waste pickers and home-based workers in Asia, Latin America and sub-Saharan Africa – sectors in which women predominate. These workers have seen their earnings fall, as demand for their products from export markets and from local people has plummeted, and increased competition is coming from new traders who have lost their jobs in the formal economy. In addition, they have also faced increasing costs, because governments have raised the fees for market stalls, and the charges for fuel, transport and utilities like water and electricity have increased.

The reproductive sector

Many women migrate internationally, to do paid care and domestic work. In these jobs, the degree of formality (in terms of documentation and protection, as well as working conditions) varies considerably. As Bina Fernandez discusses in her article in this issue, in a number of Middle Eastern countries, the official policy has been to restrict visas granted to foreign domestic and care workers. This, in a context of increased desperation for employment in the face of economic crisis at home, will inevitably result in more women entering the Gulf countries without documentation, and many more are likely to overstay their visas, leaving them to pursue informal work opportunities in the care sector, or often in the entertainment and sex industries. These strategies put them beyond the law, and any protection that might have been available from either the home country, or the country of destination (Lan, 2007).

Obviously, the vast proportion of care work takes place outside the paid labour market. In their article, Jessica Espey et al. focus on the impact of the economic crisis on unpaid care work in developing countries. The vast proportion of this work is performed by women and girls. Their article makes sobering reading; when household incomes fall, because of reductions in income and rises in food and fuel prices, the time women need to spend in earning money for the family rises, meaning the time for reproductive tasks is squeezed. This has serious consequences for the care and welfare of children, for adequate nutrition for family members, especially for women themselves, and, very importantly, for the education and health of girls, who are frequently required to supplement or substitute their own labour for that of adult women. Zoe Horn's study vividly illustrates how women suffer in these circumstances, with their own sleep and leisure time cut down as they struggle to meet the costs of school fees, health charges, as well as rent and repayment of debts.

These effects of the crisis on unpaid care work are not only a disaster for women and girls themselves, and for the children and elderly people who depend on them. It is also an issue of global concern, threatening the attainment of the Millennium Development Goals. It is clear that attaining equality in schooling between the genders, and reducing child and maternal mortality, depends greatly on what goes on in the economy. Increases in educational outcomes depend as much on freeing girls' time and energies to go to school – and the ability of the family to forgo girls' labour and to cover charges for uniforms and fees – as they do on more obviously education-related development issues, for example, ensuring adequate numbers of teachers, and constructing suitable school buildings. However, because of the invisibility of the organization of work within the household to the majority of policymakers, these concerns are often overlooked. Hence, we need not just to worry about the finance and banking sector, when we focus on the impact of the economic crisis, but also to examine the impact on production, and beyond that, the impact on the reproductive and care economy. Only by adopting this tripartite focus can we ensure that our development policies and programmes safeguard human capital and capabilities for future development.

An agenda for research and action

The articles in this volume indicate very clearly that a gender perspective on the current crisis is important for two reasons. First, it is essential that policymakers understand the different effects of the crisis on women and men. It is clear that the large-scale incorporation of women into employment in export farms, factories and services means that women's jobs are particularly vulnerable in the current economic downturn as depressed consumer spending in the global North reduces demand for exports from the South. In addition, women are primarily responsible for caring for families and dependents and hence this role comes under huge stress if there are cutbacks in state spending on social services.

Offering workers social protection

In Northern economies, workers who lose their jobs have access to some sort of social security system to cushion their economic fall, provide a (very basic) minimum income so they can survive and possibly offer them the option of training for other employment in the future. In the global South, however, there are only very rudimentary forms of social security in a few countries; and because of the nature of their work and of the local labour markets, many women workers in particular are not covered by social security entitlements, and have no cushion to fall back on. Yet, as we know, women's earnings are crucial to family well-being and children's survival.

Hence, governments and international development agencies should be looking to forms of cash transfers – whether conditional or not – which have been widely integrated by IFIs and national governments into poverty alleviation programmes, and which have provided social safety nets to counteract the worst effects of economic crisis (Molyneux, 2008; Devereux, 2006).[4]

The problems of the loss of export markets are not just problems for the macroeconomy concerned with foreign exchange balances; they are also problems of household income and human survival, which are threatened by the sudden loss of both women's and men's wages. As we have said, households which are mainly or solely dependent on women's wages are poorer to start with and have fewer resources to fall back on. Poverty-alleviation programmes which focus on (male) heads of households are a frequent response to economic decline; but in modern economies, women need cash to buy food and other essentials for their families, and this should be central to policy.

Supporting the rights to basic services

As highlighted earlier, government strategies to weather the effects of the economic crisis have focused on supporting the financial and productive sectors of the economy. However, the reproductive sector also needs support. In particular, the provision of basic services for health and education must be safeguarded. In recent decades, access to these services by people has been subject to cash inputs, which assume that families are earning sufficient income to cover this. But the economic downturn means that such cash might be less available. Development co-operation agencies, and governments, should act swiftly to ensure that poor families are able to access community and hospital health services when required, and to ensure that children, especially girls, are able to continue in school, and complete their education.

If this support does not come, women in particular will suffer stress, and mental, as well as physical, illness as they attempt to meet the needs of their dependents, as cash income is reduced, their hours of labour increase, and the cost of health and education services rises. As Jessica Espey et al. emphasize, in addition to stimulating recovery in the productive economy, it is also important to help states in the global South continue with social spending related to their commitment to achieving the MDGs, in spite of the crisis.

Short-term measures to enable communities to weather the crisis

NGOs and other aid agencies working at community level should be exploring short-term measures to help women face the immediate threat from the crisis. These might include extending and innovating in the field of micro-finance, to offer low-income families short-term adjustment loans, to ensure the survival of their businesses, and to enable their families to cover health and education charges, as well as tools and raw materials for businesses. In many countries, there is a history of women organizing communal kitchens and gardens for growing vegetables and other foodstuffs, and these should be encouraged.

Supporting women's organizations

It is also of paramount importance that NGOs are vigilant about the possible impact of the current crises on human rights of poor people. Now, more than ever, resources and energies should be given to support women's organizations, which assist members to know their rights, and to develop the capacity for effective lobbying and organizing, to hold governments to account. When there is a macroeconomic crisis, funders might be tempted to think that supporting such organizations is a luxury that they cannot afford; but it is precisely in times of crisis that such organizations are most important, since they enable women to counteract feelings of helplessness, and support women's active political participation and lobbying for measures which will help their situation. Experience from previous economic crises indicate that women become more vulnerable to personal (domestic) violence when resources for family survival are threatened, and group support is an important vehicle to support women in this situation. It is also the case that when the economy is failing, space is created for extremist political and religious organizations to flourish, which frequently do not value policies which challenge gender, class and ethnic disadvantages in the labour market, or in the family or wider community.

Researching the longer-term impact of the crisis

In the future, research needs to continue into the immediate, but also into the longer-term effects of the crisis. The crisis will also mean that many developing countries, particularly those with a high level of debt, which requires payments in foreign exchange, will be facing budgetary constraints due to loss of export earnings and the fall in value of their currencies, which makes imports more expensive. But when there is a shortage of income in the household, combined with a reduction of resources to invest in maintaining public services at an effective level, it is very often women who suffer first by going without food, and by neglecting their own health whilst being responsible for the care of other sick or elderly family members; and girl children who are withdrawn from school to assist in household tasks.

These strategies, born of desperation, clearly have very serious long-term effects. Many of these effects are directly related to gender inequality and women's rights. For example, gendered effects of malnutrition following the East Asian crisis in the 1990s are only just beginning to show. Evidence from Indonesia suggests that older people's nutrition, particularly elderly women, has suffered over the last 10 years, and stunting in children has been recorded (Thomas and Frankenburg, 2007). In countries which have historically had a strong son preference, the impact of economic crises could well make the prospects for girl children even worse, with women experiencing more pressure to abort female foetuses, with all the attendant threats that unsafe abortion poses to childbearing women and their surviving children.

The long-term health of the economy requires that the reproductive economy – the activities that go into creating healthy people who are able to work and to think and to contribute to development in the long term – are secured. This is just as important as financial balance, and maintaining employment and demand in the market economy. This is a simple but important point, if the global South is not to emerge from the turbulence in the global economy further hampered by a crisis not of its making.

Notes

1. The *Gender & Development* learning project on the Economic Crisis included a Special Issue of the journal, a Discussion Paper which came out of a learning event for development practitioners and policymakers hosted by Oxfam, at the headquarters of Oxfam GB in Oxford UK, and finally an electronic network of individuals and organizations eager to learn more about the impact of the crisis (see www.genderand development.org). Many of the articles included here emerged from papers and discussions at the learning event.
2. This refers to the consensus amongst the Washington-based institutions (including the World Bank, the IMF, the US treasury and allied think tanks in the 1990s) which insisted that the basic tenets of economic policy for developing countries should be liberalization of international trade and investment, privatization of state owned enterprises and deregulation of the private sector both in the domestic economy and internationally (Williamson, 1990).
3. Diane Elson's sentinel monitoring method is discussed in *Gender & Development* (Vol 18 No 1), pp. 143–5.
4. Conditional cash transfers (CCTs) are anti-poverty measures which are directed at mothers, in the main. Receipt of the transfer payment is made conditional on ensuring school attendance and health care for children, or participating in community health programmes or adult literacy classes. Unconditional cash transfers are payments such as old age pensions or basic income stipends, which are targeted at specific vulnerable groups. See Devereux, 2006.

Bibliography

Barrientos, S. and Smith, S. (2006) *The ETI Code of Labour Practice: Do Workers Really Benefit?*, Institute of Development Studies, University of Sussex, UK, commissioned by Ethical Trading Initiative, www.ethicaltrade.org (last accessed 1 June 2010).

Bruce, Judith (1989) 'Homes divided', *World Development* 17:7, pp. 979–991.

Cornia, G.A., Jolly, R. and Stewart, F. (1987) *Adjustment with a Human Face: Ten Country Case Studies*, UNICEF/Oxford University Press, Oxford.

Devereux, S. (2006) 'Unconditional cash transfers in Africa', *IDS in Focus*, May, www.ids.ac.uk/index.cfm?objectid=63891ABF-5056-8171-7B0C74111D63 58AC (last accessed 14 June 2010).

Dullnig, U., Neuhold, B., Novy, T., Pelzer, K., Schnitzer, E., Schöllenberger, B. and Thallmayer, C. (2010) *Taking Stock: The Financial Crisis and Development from a Feminist Perspective*. Women in Development Europe (WIDE) Position Paper on the global social, economic and environmental crisis, Vienna, http://62.149.193.10/wide/download/TakingStock_WIDEaustriaEN.pdf?id =1110 (last accessed 14 June 2010).

Evans-Pritchard, Ambrose (2010) 'Europe at risk of double-dip recession', *The Telegraph*, 24 February, www.telegraph.co.uk/finance/economics/ 7301142/Europe-at-risk-of-double-dip-recession.html (last accessed 14 June 2010).

Gaerlan, K., Cabrera, M. and Samia, P. (2010) 'Feminised Recession: Impact of the Global Financial Crisis on Women Garment Workers in the Phillipines' in Santoalla, E. L. (ed), *Gender & Development*, Oxfam: Oxford.

Garg, Ramesh, Kim, Suk H. and Swinnerton, Eugene (1999) 'The Asian financial crisis of 1997 and its consequences', *Multinational Business Review*, Fall, http://findarticles.com/p/articles/mi_qa3674/is_199910/ai_n8863181/ (last accessed 14 June 2010).

Ghosh, J. (2009) 'Will the crisis reverse global migration?', *YaleGlobal Online*, http://yaleglobal.yale.edu/display.article?id=12569 (last accessed 12 August 2009).

Hossain, N. (2009) 'Voices of the poor in the current crisis', *IDS in Focus Policy Briefing* 7.3, IDS: Brighton.

ILO (2009) *Twenty-third Synthesis Report on Working Conditions in Cambodia's Garment Sector*, ILO: Geneva.

Johnson, S. and Rogaly, B. (1997) *Microfinance and Poverty Reduction*, Oxfam and ActionAid: Oxford.

Lan, Pei-Chai (2007) 'Legal servitude and free illegality: migrant "guest" workers in Taiwan' in R. Parrenas and C. Siu Lok (eds), *Asian Diasporas: New Formations, New Conceptions*, Stanford University Press, Stanford.

Lawson, M. and King, R. (2008) 'If not now, when?', Oxfam Briefing Note, www. oxfam.org.uk/resources/policy/debt_aid/downloads/bn_g20summit%20.pdf (last accessed 7 June 2010).

McCord, A. and Vandemoortele, M. (2009) 'The global financial crisis: poverty and social protection', ODI Briefing Papers 51, August.

Mayoux, Linda (2002) 'Women's empowerment and microfinance', *UNIFEM*, New York.

Melville, Julliet A. (2002) 'The impact of structural adjustment on the poor', paper prepared for the Eastern Caribbean Central Bank Seventh Annual Development Conference, www.caribank.org.titanweb/cdb/webcms (last accessed 1 June 2010).

Molyneux, Maxine (2008) 'Conditional cash transfers: a "pathway to women's empowerment"?', Pathways Working Paper 5, Brighton, Sussex: Institute for Development Studies, www.pathwaysofempowerment.org/Pathways WP5-website.pdf (last accessed 14 June 2010).

Oxfam (2004) 'Trading away our rights: women working in global supply chains', *Oxfam International Campaign Report*, http://www.oxfam.org.uk/resources/policy/trade/downloads/trading_rights.pdf (last accessed November 2010).

Sobhani, S. and Sivakumaram, S. (2009) *The Subprime Crisis and its Implications for the Microcredit Market*, UNDP: New York.

Thomas, D. and Frankenberg, E. (2007) 'Household responses to the financial crisis in Indonesia: longitudinal evidence on poverty, resources and well-being', in A. Harrison (ed), *Globalization and Poverty*, University of Chicago Press, Chicago.

Weisbrot, M. (2007) 'Ten years after: the lasting impact of the Asian Financial Crisis', Woodrow Wilson International Centre for Scholars, www.cepr.net/index.php/publications/reports/ten-years-after-the-lasting-impact-of-the-asian-financial-crisis/ (last accessed 18 November 2010).

World Bank (2008) 'Economic crisis hits Thai workers', http://go.worldbank.org/6G1E9A9IY0 (last accessed 1 June 2010).

World Bank (2010) 'The crisis hits home: stress testing households in Europe and Central Asia', *Economic Premise*, 12, May, Poverty Reduction and Economic Management (PREM) Network, www.worldbank.org/economicpremise (last accessed 7 May 2010).

About the authors

Ruth Pearson is Professor of International Development in the School of Politics and International Studies at the University of Leeds.

Caroline Sweetman is Editor of the international journal *Gender & Development*, and works for Oxfam GB.

CHAPTER 2

The global economic crisis, its gender and ethnic implications, and policy responses

Stephanie Seguino

This chapter first appeared in *Gender & Development* 18(2), pp. 179–199, July 2010.

The global financial crisis that began in 2008 has resulted in the widespread destruction of jobs and livelihoods. Among the factors that precipitated the crisis, growing inequality both within and between countries contributed to low levels of aggregate demand and the reliance of low-income households on unsustainable borrowing to maintain living standards. The crisis provides the opportunity to rethink macroeconomic policy, and for feminist economists to advance proposals that promote jobs, economic security, and equality by class, gender, and ethnicity. Reviving the global economy will require policies that focus heavily on job creation, putting money into the hands of low- and middle-income households.

Introduction

The global economic crisis now underway has two key aspects that policymakers and governments must address. The first is the problem of a credit freeze, which has led to a virtual halt in lending for investment and consumption. The second is the dramatic decline in aggregate demand (that is, the sum of government, business and household spending), leading to extensive destruction of jobs and livelihoods.

This paper focuses primarily on the problems on the demand side of the economy – the sharp drop in spending by businesses and households that has led to massive lay-offs, first in developed and then in developing economies, further exacerbating the crisis. I also examine the gender and ethnic dimensions of these demand-side problems, and discuss policy responses that can promote rising living standards and economic growth with greater equality.

The hidden cause of the crisis: rising global inequality, and insufficient demand

A central feature of the global economic crisis that erupted in 2008, and therefore key to its long-term resolution, is the growth of inequality within and between countries. Among the numerous measures of inequality, one of the most straightforward is the ratio of income of the richest 20 per cent of households globally to the poorest 20 per cent. That ratio rose dramatically from 30:1 in 1960 to 103:1 in 2005 (United Nations Development Programme [UNDP], 2005).

Within countries at all levels of development, there is widespread evidence of growing inequality, at least since 1990. Taking the USA as an example, Figure 2.1 shows trends in family income from 1960 to 2007. The expansion of inequality is evident, with incomes of the top 5 per cent more than doubling during that period, while those of the bottom 40 per cent stagnated. Increased inequality from 1990 to 2000 is especially pronounced in central and eastern Europe and Former Soviet Republics, most Asian and Pacific economies, and advanced economies (International Labour Organization [ILO], 2008b).

One window into the problem of widening inequality is the yawning gap between wage levels and productivity growth. Increased productivity, which is the source of rising living standards, has been in evidence in many countries

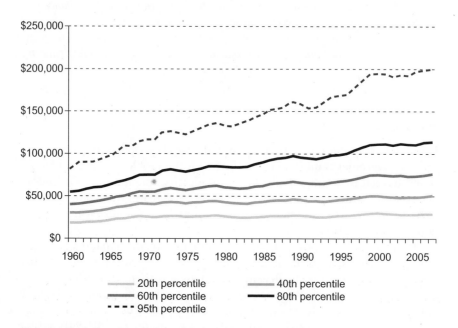

Figure 2.1 Evolution of family income in the USA, 1960–2007
Source: US Census Bureau, Table H-1, 'Income limits for each fifth and top 5 percent', all races, www.census.gov/hhes/www/income/histinc/inchhtoc.html

over the last three decades, and this should have led to rising wages and incomes. But instead, the share of national income going to workers has been falling in the USA, Europe, sub-Saharan Africa, the Middle East, Latin America and the Caribbean (ILO, 2008b). The flip side of this trend is that profits have been rising and inequality widening.

One cause of this growing gap is the increased freedom of firms and finance to move across borders. Corporations now have the option to respond to local cost pressures by relocating factories overseas, or by outsourcing production. This has undermined the bargaining power of workers and led to a slowdown in wage growth, and in some cases, an absolute decline in real wages. The fact that firms and finance are mobile has negatively affected wage growth, not only in high-income but also semi-industrialized economies (Seguino, 2007).

Women, and in many cases, ethnic subordinate groups, have been particularly negatively affected because they are concentrated in just the kinds of labour-intensive export firms that are mobile. Many low- and middle-income households have relied on borrowing to maintain their living standards, and – in the USA in particular – the consequences of this are apparent in the sub-prime mortgage crisis.[1] Unsustainable credit expansion was one way to maintain growth in the face of inequality. The wave of foreclosures (that is, the legal proceedings initiated by a creditor to repossess the collateral for a loan that is in default) in the USA, however, was a symptom of the bigger problem of stagnating incomes for workers and debt-financed consumption.[2]

This creates a macroeconomic problem: as inflation-adjusted wages fall or wage growth slows, so does workers' consumption. This has led to the central problem the global economy faces, which is one of insufficient global demand for goods and services. Without sufficient buying power on the part of workers, businesses have little motivation to invest, expand output, and create jobs.

A second and related aspect of this problem is the rise in the share of national income going to 'rentiers' (Epstein, 2005). A rentier is a person who lives on income from property or financial investments. The rise in the share of income going to rentiers, or put differently, wealth-holders, is because of high interest rates and low inflation, helped by anti-inflation policies of central banks, which have raised profits on financial investments. However, high interest rates also mean that the inflation-adjusted borrowing costs for households, small producers, and businesses have been high. This has held back job growth, further exacerbating the problem of joblessness and holding down wages. This global assessment varies by region. East Asia is an important exception to trends of falling or stagnating incomes and joblessness.

The redistribution of global income to wealth-holders and corporations suggests that a key feature of a policy to rectify the global economic crisis is one that, first, focuses on policies which promote full employment,[3] and second, seeks to resolve the problem of unequal income distribution that has led to insufficient demand. To reiterate, global joblessness is one of the central problems that macroeconomists must deal with. The most effective policy response is one that stops the destruction of jobs and sets the stage for a resumption of growth in employment, and an expansion of other livelihood opportunities.

Stratified effects of the global slowdown: gender, race, and nation

Before turning to a discussion of some responses to address employment goals, I would like to describe the trajectory of the crisis and address the gender and ethnic aspects of job losses and the credit freeze.

The slowdown, which first impacted advanced economies, has produced ripple effects on middle- and low-income countries via declines in the demand for manufactured and commodity exports, plummeting tourism expenditures, and a drop in foreign direct investment. Another channel by which developing countries are affected is the drop in remittances from family members living in developed economies. The latter may be very significant. For example, remittances to the Africa region comprise almost 2 per cent of the region's gross domestic product (GDP), and flows from developed to developing economies totalled roughly US$238 billion in 2008 (Ratha et al., 2008). While precise data on trends in remittances are not yet available,[4] anti-immigrant attitudes in Europe and elsewhere may very well lead to immigrants being targeted for lay-offs, and in any case, many immigrants work in sectors most likely to be affected by the downturn.

Employment losses and slowdowns in job growth have already contributed to substantial increases in unemployment. Many developing countries will face balance of payments difficulties since their major trading partners – the advanced economies – will continue to be in recession for some time. The loss in public sector revenues, owing to declining income tax revenues, puts downward pressure on budgets, and the effect on women will depend on whether and how carefully budget cuts are made, so as to avoid disproportionately harming women and children.

Gendered employment effects in developed economies

The effect of the economic crisis on women's and men's employment is different, but the nature of the difference varies between countries. The effects depend on whether more jobs are lost in female- or male-dominated industries. In some developed economies such as the USA, mostly men are employed in construction and durable goods manufacturing industries – the sectors hardest hit by the sharp drop in demand. As a result, to date, job losses have hurt men more than women. That said, unmarried women who head families in the USA, most of whom are single mothers, registered an unemployment rate of 12.6 per cent by October 2009, a rate that is 2.4 percentage points above the national average for all workers (Weiss and Boushey, 2009).

The unemployment data do not provide the full story of the gendered jobs effect of the crisis. As jobs are lost and income falls, fewer taxes are collected.

In the USA, most states have balanced budget rules; falling revenues can be expected to lead to budget cuts. Indeed, 48 states have budget deficits projected for 2010, with gaps through 2011 estimated to mount to US$350 billion (Center for Budget and Policy Priorities, 2010). Barring more federal spending, budget cuts and lay-offs in education, health, and other social services are likely to ensue, and indeed are already planned. Female joblessness can be expected to rise disproportionately since women workers are concentrated in occupations targeted for cuts.

In Europe, a similar scenario is unfolding. Germany expects a €316 billion tax shortfall in the next four years owing to the recession, with a number of other European countries facing similar constraints on their policy options (Buti and Szekély, 2009; Walker, 2009). The rapid rise in public sector deficits is putting pressure on governments to raise taxes or cut social spending, and if this occurs, job losses are likely to mirror those in the USA, with heavy negative effects on women's employment. Thus, a complete picture of the effects on men, women and gender relations in developed economies must include not only the short-term immediate effects of the crisis in the autumn of 2008, but also consider longer-term declines in tax revenues and resulting cuts in government expenditures in areas that affect women's employment more than men's.

Gendered employment effects in developing countries

In developing countries in which women are concentrated in export manufacturing industries (for example, Latin America and Asia), or in tourism (for example, the Caribbean), female job losses, when fully documented, are likely to be greater than male. Evidence from Thailand is consistent with this prediction (Durano, 2009). Job losses there have been overwhelmingly concentrated in the export sector; they have been especially high in electronics, an industry that employs mainly women. Employers are responding, however, in a variety of ways in addition to laying off workers. They cut wages, cut hours, delay or cut bonuses and benefits, delay salary payments, or increase overtime. As yet, gender-disaggregated data are not widely available for many of these indicators with the exception of job lay-offs. In that sense, we still have an incomplete picture of the gender effects of the crisis in terms of income from jobs.

Gendered employment and wage effects are particularly worrisome, given the large percentage of female-headed households, almost 40 per cent in the Caribbean, for example. In regions such as sub-Saharan Africa, women are mainly involved in subsistence agriculture with some off-farm work for wages or work in the informal sector. The effects of this crisis will hit this group differently than in Asia and Latin America. For the bulk of women in sub-Saharan Africa, the crisis will become apparent with the decline in remittances, and any cuts to public sector spending on education, health, and other services.

Gender norms and employment

Whatever sectors are most harmed by the economic crisis, gender norms are such that women may be fired first in some countries because men are perceived to be the legitimate jobholders when jobs are scarce. A global survey conducted in 2005 found that almost 40 per cent of respondents agreed that when jobs are scarce, men have more right to a job than women.[5] The experience of the Asian financial crisis confirmed this tendency, with women laid off at seven times the rate of men in South Korea (Singh and Zammit, 2002). We can expect this to be a dominant feature of lay-offs in a large number of countries in the current crisis.

It is also likely that in developing economies, many more women will be pushed into the informal sector as a result. In industrialized economies, women – who tend to be more concentrated in part-time employment than men – face cuts in hours of work. Official unemployment data are likely to miss this trend because, even if underemployed, women will be counted among the ranks of the employed in labour-force surveys. In developed economies, there is evidence that some unemployed women withdraw from the labour force as a response to joblessness. This, too, will result in the underestimation of the unemployment effects of the crisis on women.

Ethnic inequality

The diagnosis of the impact of the crisis needs to extend beyond the short-term focus on male and female employment. In the USA, and increasingly in Europe, the effects are likely to be racialized. Less-powerful ethnic groups and immigrants will suffer in many of the same ways women do, because they are similarly situated in the paid economy (Berndt and James, 2009). However, overt discrimination also plays a role. In the USA, by October 2009, the black unemployment rate had risen 8.2 percentage points, up from 7.5 per cent in 2007. Compare this to an increase of little more than half that amount, or 4.5 percentage points, for whites, over the 2007 average of 4.9 per cent (Bureau of Labor Statistics, 2009).

Europe's immigrants are likely to bear disproportionately the impact of the crisis, with consequent negative effects on remittances to developing countries.[6] We infer this from evidence of anti-immigrant sentiment when job availability declines. The World Values Survey (mentioned previously) found that 72 per cent of respondents believed that employers should give jobs to nationals over immigrants when jobs are scarce.[7] Europe has been much slower than the USA to document economic effects of ethnic discrimination because multi-ethnicity is a relatively new phenomenon, at least in some of these countries. While hard data on lay-offs are as yet are lacking, we know that foreign workers are concentrated in many of the hardest hit sectors. For example, 31 per cent of construction jobs in Greece are held by foreigners; 21 per cent in Spain; and roughly 15 per cent in Portugal and Italy. Durable goods manufacturing, particularly automobile manufacturing, has also been hard hit by the crisis, and similarly employs disproportionately high percent-ages of foreign workers: 23.1 per cent in the Czech Republic; 19.9 per cent in Germany; and 13.4 per cent in Italy (Taran, 2009).

The effects of the crisis on employment, combined with the ominous discussions of tax increases or budget cuts, have bolstered the political right, who made gains in recent European elections, linking anti-immigrant mes-sages to job shortages (Margaronis, 2009). In the Netherlands, the far right Freedom Party came in second; in Italy, the Northern League doubled its share of the vote; in Hungary, an anti-Roma party won 3 out of 22 seats; in Austria, 2 extreme right parties polled 18 per cent. And finally, the British National Party, at the time of the election a whites-only party committed to reversing the tide of non-white immigration, succeeded in getting two members elected to office (Margaronis, 2009).

Welfare effects by gender and ethnicity

While men are of course also expected to lose jobs, the impact will differ from the impact on women. In developed and middle-income countries, men are better positioned to weather the crisis. They have higher-paying jobs, and more assets and wealth; their jobs are more likely to offer benefits and be covered by unemployment insurance. Women's jobs pay lower wages, in part because women tend to have a higher rate of part-time employment, and are often not covered by social safety nets.

In countries without social safety nets, the impact on women is even more severe. Over half of all women in the world are in 'vulnerable jobs'; that is, they are self-employed in the informal sector, or work as unpaid family workers. Their livelihoods are thus extremely vulnerable during economic downturns (ILO, 2008a).[8] This already high percentage is expected to rise during the crisis. Female-headed households are at greatest risk, with few if any savings to weather the crisis, and limited ownership of wealth and other assets, as compared with men. Effects on the welfare of marginalized ethnic groups in developed countries mirror the impact on women. These groups have fewer wealth, assets and other resources with which to weather economic crises compared with members of dominant ethnic groups.

Jobs are the single most important vehicle for stopping the economic freefall in which many families find themselves. However, it will take seven or more years for the job market to return to pre-crisis levels. For the USA, for exam-ple, Hughes and Seneca (2009) estimate that only by 2017 will the backlog of job shortages be eradicated. Similarly, a survey of the employment effects of 80 financial crises summarized that it took three years for wages to return to pre-crisis levels, and employment seven years (UNDP, 1999). The attitudes surveys cited in this paper suggest that women and people of colour will be at the back of the very long job queue, waiting the longest to be re-employed, and yet, with the greatest constraints on surviving unemployment.

Income shocks and children

Single mothers and their children are also likely to suffer substantially because, when men experience declines in income, they are unable to contribute financial support for their children, and in particular are expected to reduce their contributions to female-headed households. During such times, women try to shield children from economic insecurity but are not able to protect them fully, on average. Lower spending power has been linked to malnutrition in children, and there is evidence that poor nutrition can have serious long-term implications for children's health and psycho-social well-being, as well as their educational achievements. Because this crisis threatens to be deeper and longer than all other crises in memory, it will require greater state intervention to support those at risk. The alternative to such expenditures is dire. The long-term costs to society of under-investment in children are well-documented.

The effect on families of the loss of income through remittances can be harsh and gendered. Studies in Uganda have found, for example, that when household incomes decline, girls are likely to be withdrawn from school, and withdrawal rates rise for older girls. Boys' education is largely sheltered from such shocks. Similar evidence of the gendered effect of economic crisis on education was found for sub-Saharan Africa in the 1980s (Björkman, 2006). It will be important in this crisis, therefore, to develop mechanisms to respond to the reduced ability of parents to send girls to school (Buvinic, 2009).

The effects on women and, therefore, children will also be transmitted through cuts in public sector budgets, owing to falling tax revenues and foreign aid. In Africa, for example, more than 50 per cent of the total public health spending comes from aid commitments. Important groups like the Global Fund to Fight HIV/AIDs, Tuberculosis, and Malaria already are facing funding shortfalls. Women who bear a huge burden for care of the sick in sub-Saharan Africa will see those pressures mount.

Responses to the crisis

A feminist macroeconomic policy stance on responses to the economic crisis should be framed around the goals of job creation, reversal of the trend of growing and unsustainable inequality, and a reduction of economic uncertainty. The mantra, simply summarized, should be 'Jobs, equality, security'. To achieve these goals, we need to do more than focus on the humanitarian goal of reducing vulnerability. We also need to promote policies that lead to structural change: policies that make equality compatible with rising living standards, and the creation of jobs, jobs, and more jobs. In short, we need a macroeconomic policy agenda capable of effecting economic and social transformation.

I discuss here several vehicles for addressing some of these goals, emphasizing ways of addressing the shortage of jobs and constraints on livelihoods. Two key strategies can help to meet the need for jobs expansion: fiscal policy (in some cases requiring assistance from advanced countries); and a reformed role for central banks.

Fiscal policy and external assistance

This crisis provides the opportunity to rethink the direction economic development policies have taken in recent years. Greater income and wealth equality – a system in which growth is compatible with equality – is a key goal. This contrasts with approaches that are dependent on inequality for growth, which have been proven to be unsustainable. How do we create the conditions for macroeconomic expansion *and* greater equality? As a first step, fiscal policies and credit allocation (discussed in more detail in the next section) should aim not only at alleviating short-run demand-side problems, but should also promote long-term growth in productivity, and arrest the growth in inequality which has been caused by neoliberal economic policies of past decades.

Stimulus packages

The poorest countries will not have the ability to engage in 'fiscal stimulus' (that is, government borrowing and spending to stimulate business and consumer spending) to generate jobs without donor funding. However, developed and middle-income countries do have the means to do so. In those cases, several criteria should guide government expenditures. Stimulus packages should not only address the contraction in consumer and business spending on goods and services. They should aim to be transformational, emphasizing three key goals: job creation; gender and ethnic equality; and a shift to a 'green' economy.

In view of this goal, governments should ensure that spending on job creation is gender-equitable. Concretely, that means governments should not just spend on physical infrastructure projects (such as building roads and construction). In most countries, the jobs in this sector largely go to men, and women would thus obtain little direct benefit of such job creation. It should be noted that India is an exception to this tendency. There, women hold a large share of jobs in such projects.[9]

Social infrastructure spending

Governments should, therefore, also allocate funding for social infrastructure investment (that is, investments in a country's most important resource – its people), in areas such as public health, education, childcare, and other social services. This has two benefits. First, it would generate jobs for women, since women are heavily represented in those occupations. Second, funding activities that help women with their care burden – for example, childcare services, contraception, and school feeding programmes – could reduce some of the negative effects of the economic crisis on women and the children for whom they care.

In countries with social safety nets, governments could also alter the rules which identify who qualifies for unemployment insurance so as to ensure women who do part-time and intermittent work are covered.

Governments should also allocate funds for apprenticeship and training programmes, in particular ones that target women for training in skilled occupations. This would help to overcome the severe problem of occupational segregation by sex that has kept women out of employment in well-paid, high-tech, skilled industries. Affirmative action programmes would also further the important goal of reducing sex segregation in employment.

In developing countries, government programming should focus on alleviating the problem of parents withdrawing girls from school. Conditional cash transfer programmes, which provide money to poor families contingent on certain behaviour such as enrolling children in school, could be expanded and increased to reduce this problem. These programmes, already in place in a number of countries (*Bolsa Familia* in Brasil and *Opportunidades* in Mexico are two well-known and successful programmes) can offer a rapid and targeted response to the crisis.

Fiscal oversight bodies

Establishment of independent fiscal oversight bodies with a quota requiring equal representation of women on them could be helpful. These bodies would monitor government spending, providing advice to ensure stimulus expenditures have an equally positive impact on women and men, and reducing the possibility of politically biased allocation of stimulus funding to dominant groups at the expense of others. Gender-responsive budgeting – that is, the allocation of funds in a way that responds to women's gendered interests and needs – is key. Women's groups are well positioned to develop proposals that will benefit women and children.

Balance of payments pressures

In some regions, such as sub-Saharan Africa, where export demand is projected to fall as a result of the decline in demand from the USA and Europe, countries will face shortfalls of foreign exchange with which to purchase imports. Some countries may respond with currency devaluations in order to spur exports. But devaluations also make imports more expensive, and the increased cost weighs heavily on women. Costs of imported food and medicines would rise in these circumstances, making it harder for women to make ends meet in the household.

There are alternative approaches to dealing with the problem of financing imports if exports decline. In the short term, countries could address the shortfall by drawing down international reserves. Estimates indicate that developing countries are holding excess international reserves equal to about 1 per cent of GDP. Using that 1 per cent to alleviate short-term current account stresses resulting from the crisis is a viable option (Rodrik, 2006; Cruz and Walters, 2008).[10] The shortfall in aggregate demand implies that counter-cyclical measures (also called 'leaning against the wind') are what are needed at this time. That is, given that the main macroeconomic problem is too little spending and thus joblessness, government policy must move in the opposite direction by increasing spending in order to counterbalance this trend. Spending reserves will provide the resource to fund increases in government spending.

Women, agricultural productivity, and food imports

In the longer term, governments in least developed countries (LDCs), especially those in sub-Saharan Africa, can address both the problems of gender inequality and balance of payments stresses by directing government funding toward resources for women farmers. Well-targeted expenditures will help women farmers increase their productivity, generating more food for families and reducing the demand for imports. Examples of ways to help women include expanding their access to credit and inputs as well as technical assistance. This strategy has big potential pay-offs. By some estimates, agricultural productivity would rise by between 10 and 15 per cent in a number of sub-Saharan countries if women farmers' access to inputs, credit and technical assistance were equal to men's.[11]

By increasing agricultural productivity, governments help to raise output and lower food prices. This reduces inflationary pressures and the demand for imports. The productivity benefits are not likely to be felt in the immediate future. However, this type of targeted expenditure that raises income over the medium to long term would be cost-effective, generating tax revenues to cover the cost of public expenditures. Moreover, investments that benefit women farmers in the short run would raise their income, helping to lessen the other negative effects of the crisis that they will experience. At the same time, government policies that help to stabilize commodity price variability can shield farmers from income volatility that is the result of fluctuation in crop yields. Responses are required both at international level (for example, through measures such as commodity price stabilization funds),[12] and at the national level via measures such as establishing agricultural market boards, most of which were dismantled under the structural adjustment programmes of the 1980s and 1990s.

Government spending on the social infrastructure of countries, aside from cushioning women and children, contributes to the long-term health of the economy by raising productivity. By directing public sector spending towards job creation and social safety nets that protect women, as outlined earlier, governments would in effect be financing development for the future, since this will have the effect of creating increased productive capacity. Seen in this way, social safety net spending has both short- and long-term benefits, serving as an investment in the country's social infrastructure and future productivity. In short, it is not only humanitarian; it makes good economic sense.

Shared employment

In cases where government budgets have to be cut, officials can implement these by reducing hours instead of cutting entire jobs. Reducing worker hours or implementing unpaid furloughs can help to support shared employment. Government can also play a leadership role, encouraging businesses to adopt a similar approach in order to avoid massive job lay-offs. As an example of this approach, South Korea's top 30 *chaebol* have cut wages of entry-level college graduates, using the savings to fund hires of additional interns and part-time workers.[13]

This method of dealing with excess workers during a crisis is preferable because it spreads the costs of the job losses more evenly across households. Although more households will have lower incomes as a result, the macroeconomic benefits are substantial. With each household losing a little income, average household saving rates will fall, but household spending will be prevented from falling further than if income losses were concentrated in a smaller number of households. This strategy also reduces pressure to fire women and ethnic minorities first.

Sources of funding

For poor countries, commercial borrowing will be more difficult to secure and more expensive. What other sources of funding to stimulate the economy are available? Official external finance will be required. Estimates by Nancy Birdsall (2009) indicate that US$1 trillion in aid is needed, and the World Bank and International Monetary Fund (IMF) currently have those resources.

Developed country governments also need to maintain their bilateral aid budgets. One of the key strategies that rich countries can adopt is to provide climate change investment support to developing economies. This kind of targeted investment can act as a substitute for the significant decline in foreign direct investment that has occurred since the onset of the crisis (United Nations Conference on Trade and Development, 2009), while also addressing longer-term global environmental challenges.

Currency transactions taxes

An option for generating revenues for the public sector that is now widely discussed is a very small currency transactions tax (CTT).[14] This source of funding has several benefits. Globally, approximately US$3 trillion is traded in foreign exchange markets daily, and only a very small percentage – less than 5 per cent – is to facilitate trade. The remainder is speculative currency transactions. This category of transaction increases financial and macroeconomic volatility, imposing costs on households not party to the transactions, especially in times of crisis. A second channel by which currency trading produces social costs is the higher level of foreign exchange reserves countries have been forced to hold to self-insure against a speculative attack. The opportunity cost of those reserves, as noted, is roughly 1 per cent of GDP that could otherwise be spent on social infrastructure to the benefit of poor households, and in particular, to reduce women's unpaid care burden.

A CTT would be similar to a pollution tax in the sense that it seeks to discourage a behaviour that can have negative social effects whose costs are not captured in the existing cost of trading, and in any case, are not fully borne by trading parties. The CTT would offer a disincentive to engage in short-term speculative transactions, and estimates of the impact on trading of a modest tax are on the order of –0.43 per cent.[15] That is, a 1 per cent increase in a tax on currency trades would result in less than a 0.5 per cent decline in trades (Schmidt, 2007). Rich countries would generate the bulk of the tax revenues, and more generally, the tax would be highly progressive. A CTT also makes tax avoidance legal and socially useful. That is, currency speculators can avoid the tax by reducing their transactions, a response that would have socially beneficial effects on macroeconomies.

Tax revenues generated from a global CTT could be pooled and earmarked for a variety of developmental purposes, including public investments in water and sanitation, a global insurance fund to respond to developing country budgetary constraints in times of economic crisis, and the Millennium Development Goals (MDGs). The project of establishing a CTT will require international cooperation, and it should be a top priority for developed countries as a means to fund social insurance, enhance macroeconomic stability, and discourage unproductive speculative financial activity by shifting the cost of the insurance to those who create systemic risk.

A global CTT could be a useful source of revenue for policies that aim to promote gender equality. Proposals for CTT rates vary, from 0.005 per cent to 0.25 per cent, generating between US$35 and US$300 billion in revenues a year. Grown et al. (2006) estimate the cost of MDG3-specific and gender-mainstreaming interventions in low-income countries at US$47 billion per year, with an expenditure stream extending for five years. That amount could easily be funded with a CTT, with remaining funds used for a global insurance fund and other agreed-upon investments in physical and social infrastructure in developing countries.

Other taxes

In all cases, addressing the demand-side problems with tax cuts for business and high-income households should be avoided. This approach will not result in significant increases in spending or job creation. The tax cuts instead are likely to be used to retire debt or will be saved with little impact on the macro-economy except to worsen budget deficits. An argument can be made, instead, for raising income taxes on wealthy households to help fund and strengthen existing automatic stabilizers – that is, social safety net programmes. Raising income taxes on this group can be justified on grounds of more evenly and fairly spreading the cost of the economic crisis, which currently is disproportionately borne by women, ethnic minorities, and more generally, the poor.

Credit policy

Governments have an opportunity to re-think laissez-faire attitudes[16] towards business investment. Instead of a hands-off policy approach that leaves business activities unregulated, governments should consider revising incentives in order to discourage speculative financial activities, and instead support businesses to make long-term investments that promote economic stability and productivity growth. A key to changing the incentive structure is to reform the role of central banks.

Reformulated role for central banks

The current crisis provides an opportunity to reconsider the role of central banks. Historically, monetary policy addressed two key policy goals, full employment and price stability. Central banks were willing to avail themselves of a wide variety of policy instruments to achieve those goals, including credit allocation techniques to fund social sectors of the economy and develop dynamic industries, and capital management to control inflows and outflows of international capital. In recent years, however, central banks have not used these instruments. They have instead narrowed the scope of their functions to focus almost exclusively on keeping inflation low; in the process, their actions have become delinked from – and often contradictory to – government policy goals.

Constraints of inflation targeting

Lack of policy coordination between governments and central banks has made it difficult for countries to stimulate investment in key sectors of the economy and address such problems as women's unequal access to credit.

The focus of central banks on inflation targeting (that is, keeping inflation low and close to zero by keeping interest rates high) has two flaws. The first of these is that inflation targeting inhibits job creation, and thus poverty reduction. That is because high interest rates used to fight inflation raise the cost of borrowing. That results in reduced spending by businesses and consumers. When buying decreases, producers cannot sell all of their goods, and employment falls. The second flaw is that many of the problems of inflation in developing countries in particular are because of supply-side bottlenecks (that is, problems which raise the costs of production such as poor transportation networks and high labour costs owing to pervasive poor health). These are problems that can be best addressed by public investment, not raising interest rates.

Moreover, evidence shows that inflation rates below 15–20 per cent do not have harmful effects on economic growth (Epstein, 2006). Inflation targeting has not only been unnecessary in some cases; it has also been socially costly. There is mounting evidence that women and ethnic minorities have suffered disproportionate job losses because of inflation targeting in developing countries and in the USA (Braunstein and Heintz, 2008; Heintz and Seguino, 2010).

Inflationary pressures are in any case receding, owing to the decline in global demand, with inflation in advanced countries predicted to fall to 0.25 per cent this year and in developing countries, from 9 to 5 per cent (IMF, 2009). It is thus an ideal moment to re-think the role of central banks.[17]

Central banks as engines of employment growth

A reformulated role for central banks should be focused on job creation. In order to expand employment opportunities, central banks could use expansionary monetary policy (that is, lowering interest rates in order to stimulate investment), development banking, and credit subsidies. To undertake this effort, governments would have to begin by outlining national goals for investment. For example, a comprehensive national investment strategy in high unemployment countries that focuses on job expansion might include subsidized credit to small-scale agriculture, small and medium-sized businesses, and large-scale businesses that can demonstrate their ability to promote significant increases in employment relative to their total spending. Women's enterprises and cooperatives could be targeted for such subsidies. The burden on the public budget will likely be limited, given women's strong track record for loan repayment. All of this implies that the set of goals outlined by the government would be linked to – and indeed, shape – the central bank's credit policy.

An example of credit policy tools that could be employed to attain the country's development goals is the combination of government loan guarantees with asset portfolio requirements – requiring banks to direct a certain percentage of their loans to targeted activities.[18] The loan guarantees would induce banks to lower their interest rates because the government had agreed to absorb some of the risk of the loans. The lower interest rate would make credit more accessible to some borrowers. Social benefits would result from directing credit to activities that stimulate job creation and raise productivity.

Capital management techniques

Central banks could also potentially help stabilize their economies through the use of capital controls (that is, policies that govern international private capital flows in and out of countries). Capital controls help reduce variability of financial flows, especially short-term speculative flows. A good example of a country that has reaped the benefits of applying capital controls is Malaysia, which was, as a result, one of the first countries to recover from the Asian financial crisis.

Financial liberalization is the root cause of volatility. Developing countries have been forced, as a consequence, to hold high levels of foreign reserves in order to self-insure against a financial crisis.[19] Reserves drain the economy by restricting the ability of governments to spend aid and loan money on physical infrastructure (such as roads and communications) and social infrastructure (that is, on investments in humans, such as spending on education and health) needed to boost the domestic economy, create jobs, and fund policies that aim to alleviate women's care burden. Capital controls help to alleviate this leakage of needed resources from the economy.

Conclusion

Many policymakers and academic economists have made the mistake of believing that unregulated markets – financial, trade, and business investment – could identify the most profitable investments, and assumed these would also be the most socially beneficial. This has not been the case. It is clearer than ever that economies require state regulation to provide incentives for private investors to align their own goals of making a profit with the social goal of creating economic and social well-being that is broadly shared across society.

A central goal of policymaking should be to shift from simply a focus on liberalizing trade, investment, and financial markets, and protection of intellectual property rights. These goals are not ends in themselves. Rather, the yardstick by which we measure the usefulness of economic policies should be their ability to generate broadly shared capabilities expansion and well-being. However, it is also clear that there is no 'one size fits all' solution to the economic crisis or development plans for long-term growth. Indeed, a major flaw of IMF and World Bank policies in recent decades has been the assumption that what is good for developed economies is also good for developing economies.

Reviving the global economy will require policies that focus heavily on job creation, putting money into the hands of low- and middle-income households. As that income is spent, rising sales will give businesses the incentive to hire workers and expand output further.

However, policies should also take a longer view. This crisis provides the opportunity to rethink the role of government and central banks in the economy. Key to effective government policy will be efforts to direct resources towards productive activity and away from speculation. Also important are measures to alleviate the downward pressure on wages that contributed to this crisis. Raising minimum wages is one strategy, though there are others.

Creating jobs will help. As unemployment drops, workers are in a better position to bargain for higher wages and more benefits, thereby generating the income to buy the goods and services that are produced. The largest share of low-wage workers is made up of women and ethnic minorities, so gender and racial/ethnic equality is likely to improve with this approach. For agricultural countries, the immediate needs are to raise productivity of farmers, especially women farmers, and finance public services such as health care and education, with targeted investments that are gender-sensitive.

This is, in many ways, a transformative moment in history, providing a window of opportunity to challenge the restrictions on economic growth and development that had been imposed by developed countries and the international financial institutions. It is an opportune moment to reconsider the view that developing countries should rely heavily on exports as a stimulus to growth. The economic contraction in rich countries, leading to a sharp decline in export demand will, in any case, force a greater reliance on developing countries' domestic demand. The policy space that has been narrowed by World Trade Organization regulations and conditionalities of IMF and World Bank loans should be revisited, and industrial policy that helps developing countries stimulate the expansion of productive capacity should be resurrected.

Addressing the economic crisis also requires a direct focus on women's well-being. Women are likely to be targeted first for job lay-offs, but typically have fewer reserves than men with which to shield themselves and their children from the drop in income. Channelling public sector spending to activities that employ women benefits not only women themselves, but also their children. It is also an investment in long-term growth. The danger in the current crisis is that governments will overlook the needs of women when deciding how to allocate funding in stimulus packages and external aid, or in making cuts. To avoid this, it is more imperative than ever that women have equal representation in decision-making on public spending, both within governments and in advisory bodies.

Notes

1. Sub-prime lending is the extension of consumer loans to risky categories of borrowers who may possess any or all of the following characteristics: low credit scores, high ratio of debt to income, or high ratio of loan to collateral. Typically the interest charged on sub-prime loans is significantly higher than the average loan rate to compensate lenders for the increased risk of default.
2. It is notable that a disproportionate share of sub-prime loans went to groups that have faced discrimination and other barriers to livelihood generation, suggesting their low income and vulnerability make them targets of predatory lending practices. See, for example, Squires et al. (2009).
3. By implication, I also include here policies that lead to expansion of livelihoods in economies where labour markets are not the primary vehicle for income generation. Such policies could include credit expansion to small businesses and farmers.
4. The Overseas Development Institute (2009) has produced a synthesis report of 10 country studies on the impact of the crisis, and cites evidence of a decline in remittances to a number of developing countries. See also Ratha et al. (2008).

5. Author's calculations from the World Values Survey, Wave 5, www.world valuesurvey.org. (last accessed 22 February 2009).
6. A recent Pew survey in the USA found that among Hispanic immigrants who sent remittances in the last two years, 71 per cent say they sent less in the past year than in the prior year. For more details, see Lopez et al. (2008). Thus far, however, the global evidence is of a slowdown on the rate of growth of remittances rather than absolute decline.
7. Author's calculations from World Values Survey data. See Note 5.
8. 'Vulnerable employment' is a newly defined measure of persons who are employed in jobs that are not waged or salaried, and thus work under precarious circumstances. This category captures work in jobs without benefits or social protection programmes. This group of workers is more 'at risk' than others during economic downturns.
9. India's National Rural Employment Guarantee Act was passed in 2005, and guarantees employment to every rural household for at least 100 days in every financial year. This is a type of employer-of-last-resort programme.
10. International reserve holdings as a percentage of gross national income have risen dramatically from the 1960s to the 1990s owing to financial liberalization (Baker and Walentin, 2001). That ratio rose from 4.7 per cent in 1976 to 27.1 per cent in 2007 (World Bank, 2008). Baker and Walentin (2001) estimate that the increase in reserve holdings has imposed an annual cost of 1 per cent of GDP on developing countries. This is because reserve holdings are invested in low interest bearing instruments such as US Treasury bonds, rather than in social and physical infrastructure investment or other higher yielding financial instruments.
11. For more details on this body of research, see Blackden and Bhanu (1999).
12. Commodity price stabilization funds are akin to 'rainy day' funds. These funds are used to stabilize the prices of internationally traded commodities whose prices exhibit a high degree of instability. The funds are used to smooth the income in the face of commodity price variability. The goal is to achieve more stable income for producers and more stable production.
13. It should be noted that the Korean Confederation of Trade Unions has been critical of this approach, arguing that the crisis is a pretext for cutting wages of regular full-time employees.
14. The CTT is now widely discussed as an option for stabilising international financial flows. The UK's then Prime Minister, Gordon Brown, publicly announced his support of a financial transactions tax at the G-20 meeting in November 2009. More recently, a campaign for a Robin Hood tax on banks has gained traction. For more information on CTT campaigns, see www.cttcampaigns.info/
15. Some have argued, however, that a very low tax is unlikely to substantially reduce currency speculation and other measures, such as capital management techniques, would be required to achieve this goal. See, for example, Grabel (2003).

16. Laissez-faire is an economic doctrine founded on a view that free markets and free trade are optimal, and that government regulation of economic activity should be limited because it leads to inefficiencies and thus waste.
17. For more on this topic, see Epstein (2003).
18. See Pollin et al. (2006) for an application of this approach to the case of South Africa.
19. Some countries such as China, however, appear to hold high levels of reserves to prevent an appreciation of their currency. This reflects their strategy of relying on exports as a vent for surplus. There are other options to export reliance. One would be to permit the currency to appreciate, and then allow domestic wages and public sector spending to increase, thereby generating the domestic demand to replace lost export sales from the currency appreciation. Women would benefit substantially from this strategy. They had been very negatively affected by the government retrenchments in previous years, absorbing a large share of the lay-offs.

Bibliography

Baker, D. and Walentin, K. (2001) 'Money for nothing: the increasing cost of foreign reserve holdings to developing nations', CEPR Policy Paper, Center for Economic and Policy Research, Washington, DC.

Berndt, J. and James, C. (2009) 'The effects of the economic recession on communities of color', Race, Health Care, and Ethnicity Issue Brief, Kaiser Family Foundation, www.kff.org/minorityhealth/upload/7953.pdf (last accessed 12 May 2010).

Birdsall, N. (2009) 'How to unlock the $1 trillion that developing countries urgently need to cope with the crisis', CGD Notes, Center for Global Development, www.cgdev.org/files/1421143_file_Resources_for_Developing_Countries_FINAL.pdf (last accessed 12 May 2010).

Björkman, M. (2006), 'Income shocks and gender gaps in education: evidence from Uganda', Job Market Paper, Institute for International Economic Studies, University of Stockholm, www.cgdev.org/doc/event%20docs/Job%20market%20paper%20M%20Bjorkman.pdf (last accessed 12 May 2010).

Blackden, C.M. and Bhanu, C. (1999), 'Gender, growth, and poverty reduction', Special Program of Assistance for Africa, 1998 Status Report on Poverty in Sub-Saharan Africa, World Bank Technical Paper no. 428.

Boushey, H. (2009) *Infographic: Gender and the Recession*, Center for American Progress, www.americanprogress.org/issues/2009/05/gender_recession.html (last accessed 10 June 2009).

Braunstein, E. and Heintz, J. (2008) 'Gender bias and central bank policy: employment and inflation reduction', *International Review of Applied Economics* 22:2, pp. 173–186.

Bureau of Labor Statistics (2009) 'Labor force statistics from the current population survey', Tables 24 and 29, www.bls.gov/cps/tables.htm#charunem_m (last accessed 1 December 2009).

Buti, M.B. and Szekély, I. (2009) *Economic Crisis in Europe: Causes, Consequences and Responses*, European Commission, Brussels, Directorate General for Economic and Financial Affairs.

Buvinic, M. (2009) *The Global Financial Crisis: Assessing Vulnerability for Women and Children, Identifying Policy Responses* Washington, DC, www.un.org/womenwatch/daw/csw/csw53/panels/financial_crisis/Buvinic. formatted.pdf (last accessed 3 March 2009), World Bank.

Center for Budget and Policy Priorities (2010) 'New fiscal year brings painful spending cuts, continued budget gaps in almost every state', www.cbpp.org/ files/6-29-09sfp-pr.pdf (last accessed 5 January 2010).

Cruz, M. and Walters, B. (2008) 'Is the accumulation of international reserves good for development?', *Cambridge Journal of Economics* 32:5, pp. 665–681.

Durano, M. (2009) 'Lessons not learned? Gender, employment and social protection in Asia's crisis-affected export sectors', paper presented at The Impact of the Global Economic Slowdown on Poverty and Sustainable Development in Asia and the Pacific Conference, 28–30 September, Hanoi, Viet Nam, www.adb.org/Documents/Events/2009/Poverty-Social-Development/gender-impact-crisis-Hung-paper.pdf (last accessed 18 November 2010).

Epstein, G. (2003) 'Alternatives to inflation targeting monetary policy for stable and egalitarian growth: a brief research summary', PERI Working Paper no. 62.

Epstein, G. (ed) (2005) *Financialization and the World Economy*, Edward Elgar, Cheltenham, UK.

Epstein, G. (2006) 'Central banks, inflation targeting and employment creation', unpublished paper, PERI and University of Massachusetts/Amherst, Department of Economics.

Grabel, I. (2003) *Currency Transactions Taxes: A Brief Assessment of Opportunities and Limitations*, www.financialpolicy.org/financedev/grabel2001.pdf (last accessed 1 March 2009).

Grown, C., Chandrika, B., Handbury, J. and Elson, D. (2006) 'The financial requirements of achieving gender equality and women's empowerment', Levy Economics Institute Working Paper 467.

Heintz, J. and Seguino, S. (2010) 'Federal Reserve policy and inflation dynamics in the US: race and gender inequalities in unemployment outcomes', Working paper, Political Economy Research Institute and University of Vermont.

Hughes, J. and Seneca, J. (2009) 'America's new post-recession employment arithmetic', Advance and Rutgers Report, Issues Paper no. 1, http://policy. rutgers.edu/reports/arr/arrr1Sept09.pdf (last accessed 9 November 2009).

ILO (2008a) *Global Employment Trends for Women 2008*, ILO, Geneva, Switzerland.

ILO (2008b) *World of Work 2008*, ILO, Geneva, Switzerland.

IMF (2009) *World Economic Outlook Update*, www.imf.org/external/pubs/ft/weo/2009/update/01/pdf/0109.pdf (last accessed 22 February 2009).

Lopez, M.H., Livingston, G. and Kochhar, R. (2008) *Hispanics and the Economic Downturn: Housing Woes and Remittance Cuts*, Pew Hispanic Center, Washington, DC.

Margaronis, M. (2009) 'Europe lurches right', *The Nation*, 29 June.

Overseas Development Institute (2009) 'The global financial crisis and developing countries: preliminary synthesis of ten draft country reports', unpublished paper, Overseas Development Institute.

Pollin, R., Heintz, J., Epstein, G. and Ndikumama, L. (2006) *An Employment-Targeted Economic Programme for South Africa*, Edward Elgar, Cheltenham, UK.

Ratha, D., Mohapatra, S. and Xu, Z. (2008) 'Outlook for remittance flows 2008–2010', World Bank Migration and Development Brief, http://siteresources.worldbank.org/INTPROSPECTS/Resources/334934-1110315015165/MD_Brief8.pdf (last accessed 18 November 2010).

Rodrik, D. (2006) 'The social cost of foreign exchange reserves', *International Economic Journal* 20:3, pp. 253–266.

Schmidt, R. (2007) 'The currency transaction tax: rate and revenue estimates', unpublished paper, The North South Institute.

Seguino, S. (2007) 'Is more mobility good? Firm mobility and the low wage-low productivity trap', *Structural Change and Economic Dynamics* 18:1, pp. 27–51.

Ajit, S. and Zammit, A. (2002) 'Gender effects of the financial crisis in South Korea', paper presented at New Directions in Research on Gender-Aware Macroeconomics and International Economies: An International Symposium, Levy Economics Institute of Bard College, 9–10 May 2002, New York.

Squires, G., Hyra, D. and Renner, R. (2009) 'Segregation and the subprime lending crisis', Economic Policy Institute Briefing Paper no. 244.

Taran, P. (2009) 'The impact of the financial crisis on migrant workers', paper presented at the ILO Tripartite Conference on Labour Migration for the Russian Federation and CIS Countries in Central Asia and the Caucasus, 22–23 June, Moscow, Russia.

United Nations Conference on Trade and Development (2009) 'Global FDI in decline due to the financial crisis, and a further drop expected', UNCTAD Investment Brief, 1 November, www.waipa.org/pdf/InvestmentBriefs/Investmentbrief_01_2009.pdf (last accessed 23 February 2010).

UNDP (1999) *Human Development Report*, UNDP, New York.

UNDP (2005) *Human Development Report 2005*, UNDP, New York.

Walker, M. (15 May 2009) 'Europe's social benefits are at risk'. *Wall Street Journal* p. A6.

Weiss, L. and Boushey, H. (2009) *The Recession Brings Higher Unemployment to Unmarried Women*, Center for American Progress, www.americanprogress.org/issues/2009/11/employment_decline.html (last accessed 9 November 2009).

World Bank (2008) *Global Development Finance*, Washington, DC, http://ddp-ext. worldbank.org/ext/DDPQQ/member.do?method=getMembers&userid=1& queryId=5 (last accessed 9 November 2009), World Bank.

About the author

Stephanie Seguino is Professor at the Department of Economics, University of Vermont, Burlington, USA, and Research Scholar at the Political Economic Research Institute, University of Massachusetts at Amherst, USA. Her research explores the macroeconomic relationship between inequality, growth, and development. Recent work develops a unified framework for understanding the macroeconomic role of race and gender inequality; explores the differential unemployment effects of contractionary monetary policy on women and ethnic subaltern groups; considers the relationship between gender and macroeconomic outcomes in countries with balance of payment constraints to growth. For the past three years, she has taught in the African Programme on Rethinking Development Economics (APORDE), a training programme in development economics for policymakers, researchers and civil society representatives from Africa and other developing countries.

The author wishes to express her appreciation to several colleagues for very thoughtful comments on earlier drafts: Lourdes Benería, Diane Elson, Gerald Epstein, Nancy Folbre, Caren Grown, Manuel Montes, and Bernard Walters.

CHAPTER 3

Gender and the global economic crisis in developing countries: a framework for analysis

Diane Elson

This chapter first appeared in *Gender & Development* 18(2), pp. 201–212, July 2010.

This chapter sets out a framework for thinking about the gender dimensions of the economic crisis. It considers the likely impact of the crisis, as well as the responses to it, on the part of both individuals and collectivities, in three spheres of the economy: finance; production; and reproduction. It identifies the kinds of 'gender numbers' that we need; sex-disaggregated statistics of various kinds. It also argues that we need to pay attention to gender norms – the social practices and ideas that shape the behaviour of people and institutions. The norms may be reinforced in times of crisis; but they may also start to decompose as individuals transgress norms under the pressures of crisis. In addition, there may be opportunities for the transformation of norms, through collective action to institute new, more egalitarian, social practices and ideas.

Introduction

A multidimensional crisis has swept over developing countries since 2007, beginning with dramatic rises in the prices of food and oil in 2007; continuing with the effects of the 'Made in Wall Street' financial crisis in 2008. This has led, in 2009, to rising unemployment, falling wages, and a slowdown in growth in some countries and an outright fall in national income in others. The form that the crisis has taken, and the government responses to it, have varied between different countries. Some had little turbulence in their finances, were able to respond with a fiscal stimulus,[1] and their growth recovered quickly. Other countries were hard hit, were unable to respond with fiscal stimulus, and had to turn to the International Monetary Fund (IMF) to borrow money in order to sustain their international debt repayments and imports. Some countries are now facing a second wave of the crisis, as falls in inflows in private finance (such as migrants' remittances and loans from international commercial banks) are accompanied by cutbacks in public expenditure, aimed at cutting budget deficits. In those countries where growth has recovered, food prices are rising again.[2]

These crises are gendered, in the sense that they have arisen out of gendered economic processes, in which women were virtually absent from key sites of decision-making in the financial sector; and in which neither private nor public finance was equitably distributed, and failed adequately to address the requirements of women as producers and as carers. The impact of these crises is gendered, too. This article presents a framework for analysis of the gender dimensions of the *financial* crisis in developing countries, for examining the impacts on, and responses of, different groups of women and men, in the context of impact on national economies, and the responses of governments. It identifies the kinds of questions it would be useful to ask, but does not aim to provide a comprehensive set of answers. The answers will, in any case, differ from country to country, varying according to the way in which a country has been exposed to the crisis, the different features of its economic, social, and political systems, and the forms that gender relations take in the country.

A gendered matrix of transmission, impacts and responses

The matrix in Figure 3.1 has three columns and three rows.[3] The columns represent economic processes, and the rows represent economic spheres.

The first column represents the processes through which the financial crisis was transmitted to developing countries. Unlike previous financial crises, such as the Latin American crisis of the early 1980s and the Asian crisis of 1997, this financial crisis originated in the 'North', principally in Wall Street and the City of London, with contributions from all the leading financial centres in the North. It arose out of dysfunctional financial innovations, which were immensely profitable in the short-run but created more and more risk in the long-run.

The second column represents the immediate impact of the crisis, following its transmission; and the third column represents the responses of governments, firms, and people.

The rows represent different spheres of the economy: the first is the financial sphere including profit-oriented banks, insurance companies, hedge funds, etc and their regulators, including central banks and Ministries of Finance. It also includes socially useful banking, such as mutual or co-operative savings and loans funds, subsidized micro-finance and state banks; and informal money lending by pawnshops, kerb-side dealers, and landlords and merchants.

The second row refers to the sphere of production, in which goods and services are produced for sale, through activities such as farming, mining, construction, manufacturing, wholesaling, retailing, and supply of leisure services, etc. This sphere includes both formal and informal paid work.[4]

Economic process / Economic sphere	Transmission from the 'global North'	Impact	Response
Finance Gender numbers Gender norms	Domestic bank problems Capital flight Devaluation Fall in FDI	Credit squeeze Fall in investment Fall in asset prices	Support for banks Direction of bank credit Controls on capital outflows Loan from IMF, World Bank etc. Reduction in borrowing
Production: formal and informal Gender numbers Gender norms	Fall in export demand	Fall in output Fall in employment Fall in earnings Fall in enjoyment of labour rights	Fiscal stimulus – selected subsidies and tax breaks Increase in people seeking informal paid work
Reproduction Gender numbers Gender norms	Fall in remittances Returning migrants	Fall in earnings Fall in nutrition Fall in school attendance	Increase in social protection transfers Cuts in social sector investment Increase in unpaid work

Figure 3.1 Matrix for analysis of gender dimensions of the financial crisis in developing countries

The third row refers to the sphere of reproduction. I define this sphere as a non-market sphere of social provisioning, supplying services *directly* concerned with the daily and intergenerational reproduction of people as human beings, especially through their care, socialization, and education. It includes unpaid work in families and communities, organized unpaid volunteer work, and paid (but non-market) work in public services like health and education.[5]

Of course, in the processes of social reproduction of the whole economic and social system, all three spheres play a role.

In each sphere, I distinguish between quantitative and qualitative aspects of gender: 'gender numbers', and 'gender norms'. By 'gender numbers', I mean the numbers of men and women carrying out different activities, as measured by sex-disaggregated statistics.

By 'gender norms', I mean the social norms that constrain the choices of men and women, and their associated social sanctions, encouraging forms of behaviour that conform to the norms, and discouraging behaviour that does not.

Some of the gender numbers and norms are very similar across all countries, while some differ considerably between countries. While men and women work in all three sectors, women's work time is disproportionately concentrated in the sphere of reproduction across all countries. In production, women and men tend to be concentrated in different occupations in different industries, but the occupations and activities seen as 'women's work' and 'men's work' vary considerably, depending on the context. For instance, in most countries, employment in construction is seen as 'men's work' and the jobs in this sector do go mostly to men; but not in India, where it is normal for women to work in construction and the industry is a major employer of women. Norms of 'male breadwinners' (or 'rice-winners') and 'female carers' tend to be strong in many countries, even if in practice women's earnings are vital to keeping families out of poverty. The responsibility to try to ensure families get enough to eat tends to be a female one in most countries, and women try to ensure that they can do this, using whatever means possible.

However, gender norms are not set in stone. In a crisis, existing gender norms may be reinforced; or they may decompose, with individual men taking on roles normally associated with women, and vice versa; or they may be transformed through deliberate collective action, by civil society groups, or by governments.

The financial sphere

The financial crisis in the global North has been transmitted to developing countries, through international markets for finance and goods. In the sphere of finance, possible transmission channels include the exposure of local banks and other financial institutions to the crisis in the North through inter-linked transactions, and participation in derivatives markets;[6] capital flight, as investors, both local and international, withdraw their capital and look for less risky investments; falls in incoming direct investment, as new investments are postponed. The currency may also be devalued if foreign currency dealers lose confidence in the currency. Those making the decisions leading to these transmission processes are likely to be overwhelmingly male – there are not many women in high finance (Young and Schuberth, 2010). The gender norms in the City of London and Wall Street are also overwhelmingly macho, encouraging competitive risk-taking, long days in the office, and after-hours drinking and visits to lap-dancing clubs (Sunderland, 2009; Kristof, 2009).

The impact is likely to include falls in investment, and in asset prices, and a credit squeeze in the formal commercial banking system, making it difficult to obtain loans for production. Gender norms will shape how this affects men and women. There may be a perception on the part of commercial banks that women are more risky borrowers, who do not provide convincing business plans. The evidence from micro-finance schemes that women tend to be better than men at repaying loans made on the basis of lending to groups of people is probably not considered relevant by commercial banks that make loans to individual businesses.

There may even be legal obstacles to women obtaining loans from commercial banks in their own right. Women-owned businesses are likely to be in a minority as holders of existing loans from commercial banks. If there is a shortage of credit, women may find it even harder than men to 'roll over' existing loans, or to obtain new loans. Thus, existing gender norms may be strengthened in commercial banking.

We must also ask how far the credit squeeze also impacts on the 'socially useful' banks and financial institutions, that do not seek to make a profits for shareholders, but to improve the lives of their users (for example, the Grameen Bank in India). Women have much greater presence as borrowers and depositors in these types of banks, particularly in micro-finance. Insofar as these institutions are not yet affected by the credit squeeze, women borrowers may be somewhat more protected than men; but the downturn or recession in growth will make it harder to market.

It is not clear how far the crisis will affect the supply of informal credit, but insofar as the crisis leads to a greater demand for informal credit, the implicit or explicit interest rates are likely to rise.

The response of governments to events in the financial sphere is likely to vary, depending on the type of regulations in place, and the extent to which there is a state banking sector. If there is any sign of a banking crisis, governments are likely to act fast, and be supported by International Financial Institutions (IFIs). But this may simply bail out the banks, without addressing the credit squeeze. The benefits of this strategy will go disproportionately to men, if most bankers and holders of bank deposits are men. If governments have instruments in place to influence the distribution of credit, then the issue is to secure a fair distribution between women-owned and men-owned businesses. Governments may be able to draw on loans from the IFIs to cover rising balance of trade and budget deficits,[7] and here the issue still remains one of the conditions attached to loans, and their gender implications. There is no evidence to suggest that the IMF seriously considers what impact the policies that it promotes have for women, men and gender equality (Elson and Warnecke, forthcoming), though the World Bank may have improved on this point, as suggested by its latest annual monitoring report on gender mainstreaming in the Bank (World Bank, 2009).

Men and women themselves may reduce their attempts to borrow, or change the reasons for which they borrow. Gender norms may influence borrowing behaviour. For instance, women may be tend to be more risk-averse than men in their borrowing for production (Elson, 2002). Such risk-aversion may be related to women's primary responsibility for ensuring the welfare of their children. An economic crisis may deepen that risk aversion. Both poor women and men may increase their demand for loans from informal financial institutions in order to finance consumption, to buy food, to pay health service fees, and so on. In doing so, they take on debt that will be an onerous burden in the future. Insofar as care for children is a disproportionately female responsibility, women may seek loans which they intend to use for consumption more than men do. Governments could prevent this by ensuring that women have access to other sources of funds (such as cash transfers).

The productive sphere

The financial crisis in the North is transmitted directly to production in developing countries via falling demand for exports (resulting from the crisis-induced recession in the North). This leads to falling output, employment and earnings in the export sectors, and, quite likely, to a deterioration in labour rights in formal employment. This in turn leads to falling demand for products intended for the domestic market, and a further loss of employment, earnings and rights. Both formal and informal employment will be affected.

The implications for women, men and gender relations depend largely on whether the export sector depends heavily on female employment (as it would if garment production was significant), or whether mostly men are employed (as would be the case in mining). In the former case, the first wave of loss of jobs, earnings and rights will affect women more than men; in the latter case, the first wave of loss of jobs, earnings and rights will affect men more than women. In occupations in which both men and women are employed doing similar kinds of jobs, such as some service occupations, then women may have greater losses than men, because of the prevalence of 'male breadwinner norms', which lead employers (and trades unions) to consider that men have more right to retain their jobs than do women. There is some evidence that this happened in the wake of the Asian financial crisis in 1997 (Elson, 2002). This reaction strengthens existing gender norms, but may be challenged by women's organizations. In South Korea, women brought unfair dismissal cases against some corporations that had pressured married women into leaving their jobs, in some cases with threats against their husbands' jobs with the same company (Lee, 2010).

However, unemployment statistics may not in themselves be a good guide to the relative impact on women's and men's employment. Women who lose their jobs may disappear altogether from the labour-force statistics, which often just include formal sector jobs, if – as in some countries – they have no rights to unemployment insurance (and thus do not register as unemployed), or because they do not go looking for another (formal sector) job because they do not expect any to be available (and thus do not count as unemployed in labour-force surveys). This does not necessarily mean, of course, that women become idle. Instead, they may take up informal employment – either home-based or street-based – of a kind that does not get captured by the labour-force statistics. In Korea after the 1997 financial crisis, official unemployment rates were higher for men than for women, even though the rate of job loss was higher for women (Lee, 2010).

Many governments have been able to respond to the impact of the economic crisis on their economies with a fiscal stimulus (i.e. an expansion of public expenditure and/or cut in taxes) that directly impacts on production via subsidies, tax breaks, and government contracts. The gender implications of this vary according to the industries favoured by the stimulus. If the favoured industries are cars and large-scale construction (for example, the construction of major roads), then in most countries, this will do more to preserve men's jobs than women's jobs. This may be appropriate, if men have disproportionately lost their jobs. But if the opposite is true, or if rate of job losses for women and men has been more or less similar, then a more balanced fiscal stimulus is called for. This could be one that targets small firms as well as large ones (insofar as small firms employ relatively more women than large firms), or one that supports the expansion of social infrastructure (such as health and education services, that we are here treating as part of the sphere of social reproduction, insofar as these services tend to employ relatively large numbers of women).

The sphere of reproduction

The direct mechanism of transmission of the crisis from the global North to the sphere of reproduction in developing countries is likely to be via a fall in remittances sent home by international migrants, and possibly a return of migrants to their families. The implications of this for women, men and gender relations will depend on the sectors in which migrants are employed overseas; and how the crisis is affecting these sectors. As in the previous analysis, if employment in traditional male-dominated industries – for example, construction – is affected more than the employment of female-dominated occupations – for example, domestic work as maids and nannies – then male migrants will tend to be worse affected than female migrants.

In addition, though, there will also be an impact on the sphere of reproduction via a knock-on from the impact on the spheres of finance and production. As a result, many households will face a loss of income. In poor families, children may become malnourished and drop out of school. This may eventually show up in statistics, but with a long time-lag. If the gender norm in a particular context is one of strong preference for educating sons, then it is likely that girls will be worse affected than boys. Gender norms of male breadwinners tend to mean that the loss of employment is particularly demoralizing for men, who lose not just a job but their sense of self-worth. In the 1997 crisis in South Korea, the government responded to this demoralization with a campaign asking women to 'Get your husband energized' (Elson, 2002). Men may respond by becoming depressed; abusing drugs and alcohol; and becoming violent, both at home and in the community.

Gender norms are also likely to suggest that it is women who must take the main responsibility for survival of household members, through increasing their unpaid work as an alternative to purchasing household goods ('make do and mend'), and through taking on casual paid work at very low rates of return. Neither the extra unpaid work nor the extra paid work undertaken by women is likely to show up in statistics; it is only revealed by small-scale qualitative research at the grassroots. In this way, even when men have disproportionately lost their jobs, it may actually end up being women who bear more of the burden of trying to provide an ultimate social safety net.

However, the loss of male employment may also lead to some decomposition of gender norms. Some men who have lost their jobs may take on more of the unpaid work of caring for children and elderly parents, especially if their wives have not also lost their jobs. There have been a few newspaper reports of this happening in the USA and UK (Qureshi, 2009; Rampell, 2009; Wylie, 2009). This phenomenon may also be occurring in some developing countries, especially middle-income countries, where both husband and wife may have formal sector jobs, and no live-in servants.

Communities may respond to the crisis through an increase in organized volunteer work, for both self-help, and to help those hardest hit. In past crises in Latin America, there have been examples of women getting together to create community kitchens, supported by aid organizations. This support may take the form of donations of food, money for small stipends, and access to premises. The crisis may reduce the provision of such support, at a time when the demand for support is growing.

Volunteer work is itself shaped by gender norms – there is a dearth of stories of men in Latin America forming community kitchens. Although men as well as women played a part in the creation of community barter markets following the 1995 crisis in Argentina, the community barter markets were predominantly a women's realm (Pereyra, 2006).

Governments can alleviate the adverse impact on communities by devoting some of the fiscal stimulus to social protection measures, such as the provision of employment or cash to poor women and men; food distribution programmes, such as school meals; waiving user charges for public services; and so on. However, it is a concern that the way in which some social protection measures are delivered reinforces, or builds on, existing gender norms. For example, cash transfers paid to mothers, on the condition that their children attend school and report to clinics for inoculations and health check-ups, have been criticized for reinforcing existing norms that make the care of children the responsibility of mothers, not fathers (Molyneux, 2007).[8] This could be avoided by removing the conditions attached to the transfers. Another example is public employment programmes that pay less than the minimum wage, such as the *Jefes* programme in Argentina, which was introduced in 2002, paying three-quarters of the minimum monthly wage to its beneficiaries, less than the cost of the basic subsistence basket for one person (Alperin, 2009). Seventy-one per cent of the beneficiaries are women, whose pressing responsibility to feed their children may lead them to accept lower pay than men are willing to accept (especially if there is any stigma attached to working for a public employment programme) (Kostzer, 2008). Women would benefit more from higher-quality programmes that pay the minimum wage, and offer some training opportunities.

Governments may also intensify the adverse impact of the economic crisis in the sphere of reproduction by cutting expenditure on services like health and education. This may happen in a secondary phase of the crisis, in which recession leads to a fall in tax revenues and an increase in budget deficits and government borrowing.[9] When this happens, it is likely to lead to an increase in the burdens on poor women, since gender norms make them primarily responsible for family well-being. This will be particularly important if health spending is cut. Expenditure cuts are much more likely if aid flows fall; and if the IMF and the financial markets prioritize a swift reduction of budget deficits and government borrowing over safeguarding the health and education of the people.

Transformation of gender norms

The crisis has opened up new spaces for changing norms about the kinds of economic policies that should be pursued. It may also open up new spaces for changing gender norms. So far, I have noted ways in which gender norms may be reinforced by responses to the economic crisis; and also ways in which they might start to decompose, owing to the individual responses of men and women. But the crisis may also provide opportunities to challenge and transform gender norms, through collective action by civil society or governments.

In the financial sphere, there is an opportunity to change gender norms in the distribution of credit to small and medium enterprises. In micro-finance, women are already major recipients of credit. Some developing country governments already play a role in determining the distribution of credit, through issuing directions to state banks, and regulations for commercial banks, which identify priority sectors for loans. Neoliberal orthodoxy frowns on the idea of directing credit providers to lend to particular kinds of clients, but the failures of market-led finance have created a more favourable climate for government and we are likely to see more of it. This provides us with an opportunity to raise questions about gendered patterns of the distribution of finance, which reflect existing gender norms about the role of women and men in society, and to persuade governments to take a pro-active role in ensuring fair shares for women. In India, direction of credit is already possible through the state banking system, which is regulated by the Reserve Bank of India (India's central bank). In December 2009, the Reserve Bank held a meeting to discuss gender issues in the allocation of credit by the formal banking system, and changes in regulations and training of officials were considered (Benita Sharma, personal email communication, 25 December 2009).

Stimulus packages provide another opportunity for changing gender norms. States could require particular industries to open up particular occupations to women, as a condition of receiving finance. These occupations could be ones in which women are currently under-represented. Measures could include the provision of training opportunities, policies to make workplaces more women-friendly, and targets for increasing the employment of women. As yet, no stimulus package appears to have taken this opportunity.

Volunteer organizations could take steps to mobilize more men for the kind of care work that is currently done mainly by women. This had begun prior to the crisis, in some volunteer programmes in Africa that provide care for people living with HIV. In many cases, the volunteers are given small stipends, which are not wages set at market rates, but a money allowance that covers some of the expenses of volunteering, and provides tangible community recognition of care as valuable work. One study, in South Africa, found that the stipends are important in attracting male volunteers, and concluded that: 'An increase in the stipends may help enhance recruitment of males to care-giving' (Kgware, 2006: 12). This merits further investigation as a way of changing gender norms.

Conclusion

The purpose of this article was to suggest a framework for thinking about the gender dimensions of the economic crisis. The framework that I have suggested enables us to examine the impact of the crisis, as well as the responses to it, on the part of both individuals and collectivities, in three spheres of the economy: finance, production, and reproduction. It identifies the kinds of 'gender numbers' that we need: sex-disaggregated statistics of various kinds, and data which enable us to plug existing gaps in our knowledge, since the data the governments regularly produce still continue to leave out women's unpaid work and much of their informal paid work. The article has also argued that we need to pay attention to gender norms – the social practices and ideas that shape the behaviour of people and institutions. The norms may be reinforced in times of crisis, but they may also start to decompose as individuals transgress norms under the pressures of crisis. In addition, there may be opportunities for the transformation of norms, through collective action to institute new social practices and ideas.

As the first wave of the financial crisis recedes in many parts of the world, the other dimensions of the crisis, especially shortages of affordable food and fuel, will come to the fore. A similar framework, with appropriate modifications, may prove useful in considering the gender dimensions of these crises.

Notes

1. Fiscal stimulus refers to a policy of stimulating the economy by compensating, in whole or in part, for a fall in expenditure by households and businesses, by an increase in public expenditure and/or a reduction in taxes.
2. In countries in which economic growth has recovered food prices have risen again because of the fact that demand has risen but the underlying constraints on the supply of food have not been addressed.
3. The matrix in Figure 3.1 draws on my presentation to the Oxfam Gender and Economic Crisis Workshop, Oxford, in September 2009, modified slightly in light of subsequent discussions. I particularly thank Ruth Pearson for her comments. The changes that I have made differ somewhat from those made by King and Sweetman (2010), who also present a modified version of my framework.
4. Unlike King and Sweetman (2010), I do not include informal paid work in the sphere of reproduction, even though some of it may be home-based. Since it is paid and produces products that are sold on the market, I include it as part of production. Through sub-contracting, some informal work contributes to the products of large-scale producers, including those that produce for export.
5. Some authors adopt a narrower definition of reproduction, which includes only the unpaid activities undertaken within households. However, I consider that provision of public services is 'non-market work', because public services are not produced for the market, even when there is a service charge for users. This is because user charges for public services are taxes, rather than prices; they are not set by interaction of supply and demand in a market, or by an enterprise based on what will maximize profits.
6. Derivatives are complex financial instruments which are derived from some other instrument, such as loan to a person to buy house, or to a business to buy equipment, or to a government to build a bridge. They are traded between financial institutions and their values become divorced from the value of the underlying investments.
7. Balance of trade refers to the gap between the value of imports and exports. If the value of imports is greater than the value of exports, then there is a trade deficit.

8. Such programmes had been widely adopted in Latin America prior to the crisis.
9. Since I consider expenditure cuts a response to the crisis, I do not place them in the matrix in the column for transmission of the crisis. Here I differ from King and Sweetman (2010).

References

Alperin, M. (2009) 'The impact of Argentina's social assistance program on structural poverty', *Estudios Economicos* pp. 49–81, Numero Extraordinario.

Elson, D. (2002) 'The international financial architecture – a view from the kitchen', *Femina Politica – Zeitschrift für feministische Politikaissenschaft* 11:1, pp. 26–37.

Elson, D. and Warnecke, T. (forthcoming) 'Gender and macroeconomic policy rules: the case of the IMF poverty reduction and growth facility', in B. Young, I. Bakker and D. Elson (eds), *Gender and Macroeconomic Governance*, Routledge, Abingdon.

Kgware, M. (2006) 'Men as carers: a case study', unpublished paper, Oxfam Australia.

King, R. and Sweetman, C. (2010) 'Gender perspectives on the global economic crisis', Oxfam International Discussion Paper, Oxford.

Kostzer, D. (2008) 'Argentina: a case study on the *Plan Jefes y Jefes de Hogar Desocupados* or the employment road to economic recovery', Working Paper no. 534, The Levy Economics Institute of Bard College, New York.

Kristof, N. (2009) 'Mistresses of the universe', *The New York Times*, www.nytimes.com/2009/02/08/opinion/08kristof.html (last accessed 4 June 2010).

Lee, J-Y. (2010) 'Restructuring women's employment in South Korea, 1997–2005: the role of the state and NGOs', PhD thesis, University of Essex, UK.

Molyneux, M. (2007) 'Change and continuity in social protection in Latin America. Mothers at the service of the State?', Working Paper 1, UNRISD, Gender Development Programme, Geneva, Switzerland.

Pereyra, F. (2006) 'Experimenting with community currency schemes in Argentina: an analysis of the market from the perspective of economic sociology', PhD thesis, University of Essex, UK.

Qureshi, H. (24 October 2009) 'New female breadwinners', *The Guardian*.

Rampell, C. (6 February 2009) 'As layoffs surge, women may pass men in job force', *The New York Times*.

Sunderland, R. (2009) 'We cannot return to the old macho ways', *The Guardian*, www.guardian.co.uk/business/2009/feb15/gender-recession-credit-crunch (last accessed 4 June 2010).

Young, B. and Schuberth, H. (2010) 'The global financial meltdown and the impact of financial governance on gender', Garnet Policy Brief no. 10.

World Bank (2009) 'Implementing the bank's gender mainstreaming strategy', FY08 Annual Monitoring Report, World Bank, Washington, DC.

Wylie, I. (2009) 'Redundancy: how to restore balance', *The Guardian*, www. guardian.co.uk/money/2009/sep/26/redundancy-restore-balance (last accessed 4 June 2010).

About the author

Diane Elson is Professor of Sociology at the University of Essex, UK.

CHAPTER 4

Critical times: gendered implications of the economic crisis for migrant workers from Burma/Myanmar in Thailand

Jackie Pollock and Soe Lin Aung

This chapter first appeared in *Gender & Development* 18(2), pp. 213–227, July 2010.

This chapter draws on the grassroots experiences and research of MAP Foundation to examine the gendered impacts of the economic downturn on migrants from Burma/Myanmar[1] who are working in Thailand. The chapter looks through a gender lens at the wages, working conditions, family relations and safety and security issues. It finds that migrant women have experienced decreases in wages, lay-offs, increased restrictions on reproductive rights and increased risks of harassment and extortion as a result of the economic downturn. It also finds that the usually resilient Burmese migrant communities are being stretched beyond their limits, and need urgent protection.

Introduction

On December 18, 2008, the International Labour Organization (ILO) released a statement marking International Migrants Day. In it, Juan Somavia, Director General of the ILO, spoke of the global economic crisis, in relation to migrant workers:

> The current global financial and economic crises have serious implications for migrant workers worldwide. Past experience makes us painfully aware that migrant workers, especially women workers and those in irregular status, are among the hardest hit and most vulnerable during crisis situations. While the full impact of the crisis on migrant workers is yet to unfold, there are reports of direct layoffs, worsening working conditions including wage cuts, increasing returns, and reductions in immigration intakes.
> (Somavia, 2008)

At that time, the economic crisis was just a few months old. Only considerably later would the United Nations (UN) General Assembly call it, 'the worst financial and economic crisis since the Great Depression'.[2] Yet, even at this early point, Juan Somavia already saw fit to draw special attention to the situation of migrants in the economic crisis, and the situation of women and irregular migrants[3] in particular.

In Thailand, the heavily export-oriented economy left the country inordinately exposed to adverse macroeconomic impacts. With exports accounting for more than 65 per cent of gross domestic product (GDP), it can be little surprise that by the first quarter of 2009, the Thai economy had already contracted 7.1 per cent since the previous year. This was particularly significant for migrant workers, who are employed in large numbers in the garment manufacturing industries, the seafood export industry, and the vast orchards and plantations that are the source of fruit, rubber, vegetables for many countries around the world.

This chapter draws on the grassroots experiences and knowledge of the MAP Foundation, a Thai non-government organization (NGO) that was founded in 1996. MAP Foundation aims to improve the rights of migrant workers from Burma/Myanmar who are working in Thailand. It focuses particularly on the labour rights of domestic workers, factory workers, construction and agricultural workers.

The chapter draws on research published as a report, entitled *Critical Times* (Aung and Aung, 2009), which explored the gendered implications of the economic crisis on migrant workers in Thailand. The research involved 374 migrants from Burma/Myanmar who are working in Mae Sot. Most are employed in sectors of the economy which produce goods for export, and are dependent on foreign direct investment.

Our research aimed to find out about the impact so far of the economic crisis on migrant workers and their families. In particular, we were interested in how its effects differ for women and men. The analysis here focuses on these concerns, and in particular explores how they are playing out in Mae Sot, Tak province. Mae Sot is an increasingly industrialized district, on the Thai-Burma border. It provides a good case study for this article, owing to the profusion of export-oriented garment and textile factories, with a mainly female workforce and because MAP Foundation works closely with the migrants in this area to support the formation of migrant workers associations which can address the pervasive exploitative conditions, to provide legal assistance for migrants pursuing complaints of exploitation by their employers and to advocate for full protection of rights of migrants. The research involved a combination of qualitative and quantitative research methods: four focus group discussions (with a total of 28 migrants); 15 in-depth interviews; and a survey with 331 migrants which took place between June and August 2009. To protect the confidentiality of the migrants who took part in our research, we have not used their names in this chapter.

The context: Burmese migrant workers in Thailand

The 2009 UN Development Programme (UNDP) report 'Overcoming Barriers: Human Mobility and Development' explains the pull for migrants from Burma/ Myanmar stating that: 'Someone born in Thailand can expect to live seven more years, to have almost three times as many years of education, and save almost eight times as much as someone born in Myanmar [Burma]' (UNDP, 2009: 9). Most estimates suggest that there are between two and three million migrants from Burma/Myanmar, Cambodia and Lao PDR working in Thailand, over 80 per cent are from Burma/Myanmar. Only figures for migrants who register once they are in Thailand and apply for the temporary work permits are available. The number of migrants applying for these work permits has fluctuated, from 300,000 in 1996, to 1.28 million in 2004, decreasing over the following years and increasing to 1.3 million in 2009.[4] These numbers reflect the accessibility of the registration policies rather than the actual number of migrants.

The vast majority of migrants from Burma/Myanmar arrive in Thailand without any form of documentation. Thailand first responded to this situation in 1992 (World Bank, 2006; Huguet and Punpuing, 2005) with policies which allow Burmese migrants already in the country to register to work for a year at a time. These policies are intended for 'migrants who entered the country illegally' to register to work for one year 'while awaiting deportation' (translations of the wording in the Royal Thai Government Cabinet Resolution, 25 June 1996). Despite the temporary nature of the policies, workers have been able to renew them annually for nearly two decades.

In 2003, the Burmese regime signed a Memorandum of Understanding (MOU) with Thailand to regularize migration. However, it took the next six years for the two countries to come to an agreement on how to implement this MOU. In 2009, the Burmese regime set up offices in three locations along the border, in Tachilek, Myawaddy and Kawthuang to interview migrants who had been working in Thailand to verify their nationality and issue temporary passports.

In looking at the various effects of the global financial and economic crisis on migrants and their communities, we not only have to understand that these are different for women and men, but we also need to recognize how global capital actually perpetuates and causes inequality between women and men by the ways in which it shapes the lives and work of migrants:

> Perhaps the most notable feature of female migration is the extent to which it is founded upon the continual reproduction and exploitation of gender inequalities by global capitalism. For the most part, female labor migrants perform 'women's work' as nannies, maids, and sex workers – the worst possible occupational niches in terms of remuneration, working conditions, legal protections and social recognition. In this way, gender acts as a

basic organizing principle of labor markets in destination countries, reproducing and reinforcing pre-existing gender patterns that oppress women. (UN International Research and Training Institute for the Advancement of Women [UN-INSTRAW], 2007: 3–4)

Migrant women who meet monthly to share experiences in 11 different locations along the Thai-Burma/Myanmar border in the Women Exchange programme organized by MAP Foundation, say that Thailand offers them a mix of opportunities and threats. The opportunities include paid work, access to healthcare, the possibility of official protection under the labour laws, and exercising other rights. The threats, on the other hand, include poor occupational health and safety conditions, which may result in death or injury; the constant fear of arrest and deportation; debt-bonds to employers, and dependency on informal brokers. The migrant women also relate their feeling of being deliberately isolated, whether it be as a domestic worker with no legal protection guaranteeing days off to meet their friends, or as factory workers housed in dormitories behind the closed gates of the factory, or as construction site workers living in shacks on the site. These arrangements are, in their understanding, condoned by the authorities.

In the next section, we explore in greater detail migrant women's experiences of working in Mae Sot during the economic crisis.

Mae Sot and women's work experience there

Mae Sot is a district on the Thai-Burma/Myanmar border in Thailand's Tak Province. Owing to its geographic proximity to Burma/Myanmar, Mae Sot has long been a major destination for migrants leaving the country to work in Thailand. Numbers of migrants in Mae Sot increased in the mid-1990s when the town became a production centre for garment factories (Macan-Markar, 2003). The combination of rapid industrialization and the presence of a highly mobile labour reserve has not had a positive effect on local employment conditions. Indeed, the large pool of non-unionized labour to be found in Mae Sot appears to be an attraction to both the local and foreign companies.

Thailand continued to develop economic corridors based on Greater Mekong Subregion and ACMECS[5] schemes. According to the Economic Cooperation Strategy (ECS) initiated in 2003, Mae Sot belongs to the East West Economic Corridor (EWEC) which promotes trade and investment with Burma/Myanmar. On 19 October 2004, the Thai cabinet decided to create a border economic zone in Tak province, covering three districts of Mae Sot, Phop Phra and Mae Ramat. On 6 October 2009, the Cabinet approved the Ministry of Commerce's project to develop the special economic zone, which also consists of a one-stop service centre and logistics park (Government Public Relations Department, 2009). The Tak Chamber of Commerce has called for incentives to attract industries such as garments, textiles, ceramics and furniture. There are currently an estimated 300 factories in Mae Sot, which it is speculated may be expected to relocate to the proposed industrial estate (Tsuneishi, 2007). Each of the factories employs between 100 and 1,000 workers, while about another 200 unregistered 'home factories' would employ between 5 and 20 workers (Kusakabe and Pearson, 2007).

For Thailand, this economic co-operation is tied to its own internal regional development. By shifting agriculture and labour-intensive manufacturing to border economic zones along the corridors, Thai industries can benefit from cheap labour and resources from neighbouring countries, while the neighbouring countries can benefit from job creation and the development of consumer markets.

The history of the industrialization process here is also a history of the continued suppression of labour rights. In a press interview, Phil Robertson, head of the Thai office of the American Center for International Labor Solidarity, a Washington, DC-based international NGO, judged Mae Sot to be 'the cesspool of labour rights of Thailand. All labor laws are violated ... You find the most systemic oppression of workers in Thailand' (Macan-Markar, 2003). Other observers for example, Pongsawat (2007) and Sang Kook (2007), see the suppression of labour rights in Mae Sot as part of an active campaign on the part of public and private actors to encourage and consolidate investment in the area. According to Arnold and Hewison (2006), employer organizations such as the Chambers of Commerce or the Federation of Thai Industries (FTI) actively constrain the action of workers, particularly by limiting freedom of association and colluding to maintain low wages.

These local conditions combine with national restrictions on migrant workers, which include severe restrictions on the right to travel, or change employers, and the restrictions in the Thai Labour Relations Act B.E. 2518 (AD 1975) on non-Thais holding any official position in a union. Thus, migrants are effectively banned from forming their own unions or travelling to meet and join Thai unions. Since 2007, the Action Network for Migrants (Thailand) has been working with the Thai Labour Solidarity Committee (TLSC) initially to introduce Thai workers to migrant workers issues, and more recently to facilitate migrant workers joining Thai unions.

Apart from labour law violations, migrant workers' lives are also made insecure and precarious by laws and policies which make it much easier and simpler for a migrant to lose their legal status than to gain it. MAP Foundation facilitates monthly meetings of workers, at these labour exchanges, workers report how employers confiscate their work permits, which exposes all migrants to extortion by the police and for women migrants also exposes them to sexual harassment from immigration and police officers when they cannot produce their documentation. As noted previously, with the economic downturn migrants have to move more frequently to find work, but since migrants are not allowed to travel, this situation again increases their risk of arrest and deportation.

Since the first landmark case of migrant workers of the Nut Knitting Factory in Mae Sot winning compensation of around £1,000 each in 2004 (MAP

Foundation, 2006), MAP Foundation has provided paralegal assistance to over 1,000 migrants each year in Mae Sot for unpaid wages and exploitative working conditions. Seventy per cent of these workers are women and face particular harassment when they first start to make a complaint. During the legal processes, MAP Foundation, together with our local partner, the Yaung Chi Oo Workers Association, have been called on to respond to situations where the women workers leaders have been abducted and threatened, thugs have been sent into their dormitories at night and they have been arrested and deported. According to information provided to MAP Foundation's grassroots programmes with women workers, general campaigns of intimidation are waged against women workers who dare to organize and demand their labour rights.

In the next section, migrant women talk about how they experienced the economic downturn in Mae Sot and how it impacted on their lives.

Gendered impacts of the economic downturn

Given the high concentration of export-oriented industries in Mae Sot, it can be little surprise that the current economic downturn has produced severe negative impacts for Mae Sot's factories, and in particular for the migrants and their families, whose livelihoods depend on them. Knitwear factories, which produce warm clothing largely for very hard-hit US and European markets, are said to be struggling disproportionately, with demand dropping steeply alongside Thailand's broader 26.5 per cent year-on-year contraction in export earnings (Moe Swe, Yaung Chi Oo Workers' Association, interview, 14 August 2009). In Mae Sot's factories overall, orders have dropped across the board. The local chapter of the FTI claims that orders have dropped by 12 per cent (*The Economist*, 2009).

Wages

In Mae Sot, in general single men and women work in factories, while family units work in agricultural areas and on construction sites. A few factories have special dormitories for couples and even fewer say they provide facilities to families. According to reports from workers in Mae Sot, these latter factories are often the most exploitative because the families have so few choices. In agricultural and construction sites, women workers are paid much less than the men workers; while in the sectors where the majority of workers are women, such as textile factories or domestic work, the wages are kept low. Thailand has a legal minimum wage, which employers must pay all workers, regardless of their immigration status. Thailand's Constitution also lays out anti-discrimination policies between men and women. Nevertheless, migrant women are receiving less than the minimum wage and less than men for the same job; this was the reality before the economic downturn and will very likely outlast it. This helps explain the way in which the downturn appears to have aggravated gender inequalities in pay-scales within Mae Sot's migrant communities. At the launch of the report, *Critical Times*, (Foreign Correspondents Club Thailand, September 2009), one of the panellists, Tim De Meyer, labour standards specialist in the ILO, said that: 'All too often migrant workers in poorly visible categories of work tend to be the shock absorbers during an economic downturn', and that the ILO had the female migrant workers from Myanmar in mind when it said earlier that year that the current economic meltdown had a 'woman's face' since women labourers are affected more severely, and differently, compared with their male counterparts.[6]

Our research shows that the economic downturn has worsened wages for workers. According to MAP Foundation's research, only slightly more respondents – 43.8 per cent – reported a year-on-year decrease in income, compared with 42.7 per cent who reported no change to their income. However, compared with this, a full 85 per cent of respondents reported finding themselves in difficulty owing to being unable to afford goods which are rising in price. Migrants reported explicitly that year-on-year wages had fallen significantly in real terms. High-season earnings in 2008 for a knitting factory employee would have been around US$180 per month, and US$90 per month for garment factory workers. A year later, all factory workers were reporting an average of about US$75 per month.

In many different parts of our research – through surveys, written statements, focus-group discussions, and in-depth interviews – migrants consistently drew attention to a growing gap between wages and goods prices when describing their economic difficulties. Even an income that has not changed will be associated with increased daily struggle, while an outright decline in income spells a serious and increasing threat.

Analysing our research findings by gender and employment sector revealed significant difference in the situation of women and men. Women are considerably more likely than men to report falling income – 47 per cent of women, and 39.1 per cent of men, reported declines. Factory work has seen negative changes in wages, with 57 per cent of factory workers reporting an outright decline in income:

> At this time wages are so low. I just get 30 to 90 baht [US$0.9–2.7] per day. And spending costs have increased, so I cannot save money right now. (Knitting factory employee [female]; Aung and Aung, 2009: 26)

Households, and extended families in Thailand and Burma/Myanmar, who depend on female wages are struggling most to make ends meet in the face of the crisis In other income-related findings, a majority of respondents – 67 per cent – reported that they were finding it increasingly difficult to save money, and even more – 72.2 per cent – were finding it increasingly difficult to support their families. Women were more likely than men to report savings difficulties, as were factory workers compared with workers in all other sectors.

The economic crisis is creating conditions in which women workers, who are already are relatively undervalued and underpaid because of gender stereotypes about the sectors in which they are employed, find that wages are being affected worse than those of men in other 'masculine' employment sectors. Sector-specific economic effects of the crisis – on export-dependent textile factories especially – map onto gender-specific impacts with troubling clarity. In Mae Sot, the suffering of certain industries can hardly be separated from the suffering of the women migrants who disproportionately work in them.

With fewer savings, migrants reported a drop in the levels of remittances to their relatives inside Burma/Myanmar. This has also been compounded by an unfavourable increase in the exchange rate of the *kyat* Burmese currency against the *baht* Thai currency. Migrants reported that usually they sent remittances home quarterly or yearly, and thus the hardships which migrants experience immediately when their wages fall and purchasing power decreases are not immediately passed on to the communities back home; rather, the hardships will ripple down over the following year:

> Over 30 people have come to work in Thailand from my village. There are six people in my village that are depending on the money I remit home. Earlier I could remit money four times a year; now I can only send twice a year. (Ms Deng Lungiong, 26-year-old Shan domestic worker speaking on the panel at the launch of the *Critical Times* report at the Foreign Correspondents Club Thailand, September 2009)

> I can't support my parents because I'm not in a good job situation. My brother and sisters are also not OK – they also can't support with any money. Sometimes, we argue with each other.
> (Survey 2, ID 6, carpenter [male]; Aung and Aung, 2009: 27)

> If I cannot send money to parents, they have to face health problems and social problems, and they have difficulty with daily costs.
> (Survey ID 68, knitting factory employee [male]; Aung and Aung, 2009: 29)

Unable to support their families and barely able to support themselves, migrants in Mae Sot have to make difficult decisions regarding their future. The vast majority of those workers interviewed for this research – 95.4 per cent – reported that they would rather stay in Mae Sot during the economic crisis than return to Burma/Myanmar:

> I have been living in Mae Sot for four years. My economic situation is not okay now. Income and spending are not balanced. Therefore, even if I want to go back to Burma, I cannot go back. So I am very depressed.
> (Survey 2, ID 14, female factory worker)

During one of the initial discussions about the research with a group of migrants in Mae Sot, they reported that some women who had been dismissed from factories had returned to Burma/Myanmar with a broker who was organizing for them to travel to Jordan for work in factories. Later, 500 of these women who were working in a Chinese factory in Irbid, Jordan contacted MAP Foundation when there was a labour dispute.[7]

Working conditions

The suppression of labour rights in Mae Sot discussed earlier is important in understanding the impact of the economic downturn on migrant workers in Mae Sot; the conditions are already so poor that there is very little scope for deterioration.

The question of working hours is quite complicated, owing mostly to distinctions between workers, who are categorized by employers into those workers whose skills are valued (referred to as 'skilled'), and those whose skills are not perceived and hence unvalued (referred to as 'unskilled'). Women's jobs are more likely than men's to be classed as unskilled or semi-skilled. In a textile factory, the machine work on the shop floor is considered unskilled work, while the workers who make the samples for orders, who make designs or work on complex designs and the foremen are called skilled workers.

According to MAP Foundation's research, the impact of the economic crisis was complex. Working hours for the 'unskilled' declined year-on-year during the middle quarters of 2009. It was these workers who were most likely to be dismissed because of worsening economic conditions. As orders declined, the numbers of workers needed on the shop floor decreased and the workers are immediately dismissed. Should orders increase, the factory has a large pool of workers in Mae Sot looking for jobs that they can employ and dismiss as needed. In contrast, factories prefer to keep their skilled workers on the payroll than dismiss them and risk them using their skills (for example, in design or sampling) in another competing factory. While waiting for new contracts, skilled workers work on the shop floor to fill the shortages created by the dismissal of the supposedly 'unskilled' workers. Low-skilled workers in Mae Sot, as we have seen, are both more likely to be women, and more vulnerable to retrenchment when economic conditions threaten the financial security of their employers. Because they are disproportionately numbered among the workers considered low- or unskilled, women were more likely than men to find their working hours decreased, including overtime hours. Working long hours is essential if migrants are to be able to save.

Interestingly, a different dynamic was reported by some skilled workers who said their working hours had increased, rather than decreased, as a result of the economic crisis.

Despite reportedly steep declines in production, the fact that there were now fewer employees resulted in those who remained gaining more hours on the factory floor.

Interestingly, migrants in Mae Sot were not convinced that either the lowering of wages or the laying-off of workers was always directly linked to the economic downturn. This is supported by the history of suppressing labour rights, referred to earlier. It had been no surprise for the workers in Mae Sot to find that notices declaring that the factory was closing because of the economic crisis were posted at factories where workers were making complaints about decreasing wages or deteriorating working conditions. The workers' scepticism is well-founded; in more than one instance, a business which had apparently crashed financially, re-opened just down the road under a new name and of course, with a new, unversed in labour rights, set of migrant workers (discussions between workers and MAP Foundation and Yaung Chi Oo Workers Association volunteers, August 2009).

In Thailand, the Labour Laws are said to protect all workers, regardless of their immigration status. These laws specify severance pay packages for workers who are laid off in such circumstances. Nevertheless, no migrant worker has yet received an official redundancy package. The vast majority were notified of the loss of their jobs on the day they were required to leave, and were sent away without even the wages owed to them.

> They told us to pack up and leave. I heard someone ask for their wages and the foremen shouted that he was ready to call immigration if anyone wanted to make a complaint. We all hurried to pack up our things.
> (Discussions between MAP Foundation staff and female factory workers in Mae Sot, August 2009)

The study's results for working conditions were among the least conclusive findings generated. Intuitively, the decline in factory earnings in Mae Sot would lead to a deterioration in working conditions. However, this is not reflected in our findings. Of the respondents, 71.9 per cent in fact reported no change from the previous year in general working conditions, and the remaining 28 per cent who did report changes were roughly split between reports of deteriorating conditions, and improved conditions, again this is a statement on the general working conditions that are the norm in Mae Sot.

Impact of the economic downturn on family dynamics

Our research exposed little noticeable change in family dynamics that could be linked to the economic situation. However, it is significant was that only 67 per cent of those surveyed chose to respond to this question. This may, however, be because of shortcomings in our research methods: migrants may well have been reluctant to get into discussions about family relationships and sensitive issues including domestic violence in mixed-sex groups and formal research settings, including interviews and focus groups. Several organizations in Mae Sot offer support and refuge to survivors of domestic violence, but it is difficult to see any changes in reported violence which can be linked to the economic crisis.

The economic crisis has, however, visibly put further strain on migrant families who have children in school. While the implementation of the UN Education for All policy in Thailand permits all migrant children to attend free state schools, there are costs involved for the parents, including paying for transport to the schools, school uniform, books, and so on. Migrant families on agricultural and construction sites reported to the Rights for All project of MAP Foundation that, with decreases in salaries, they were only able to keep one child at school. When the families had one son and one daughter, they reported that they were more likely to take the daughter out of school, reasoning that she could help the family at home. These families also reported that their mobility had increased as a result of the economic downturn, as they had to move more often to find work, increasing instability for the family, and often resulting in the children not being able to attend school regularly:

> All our community had wanted was for our children to go to school. We asked MAP to help organize that to happen a couple of years ago, and we were so excited when they went to school. But now, many families are taking the children out of school. Our community lives far from the school and we are always a little scared when the truck comes to pick up the children, now we either don't have the money or are even more afraid that the children won't be returned at the end of the day.
> (Discussion between MAP Foundation staff and agricultural workers on Mae Sot-Phop Phra road, August 2009)

With decreased incomes, migrant couples are faced with dilemmas regarding planning their families. Many migrant women from Burma/Myanmar have been or will be in Thailand for the best part of their reproductive life. It is only in recent years that the babies of migrants could obtain a birth certificate, and registered migrant women have been entitled to general health care, including limited reproductive health care such as contraception.

Nevertheless, when women are pregnant and cannot work, they immediately lose their jobs and their housing, which is, as mentioned earlier, linked to their work. Such restrictions mean that women have few options and may result in unsafe abortions,[8] excessive use of the emergency pill, unemployment and lack of livelihood for mothers. They are also likely to breed resentment among the migrant community, whose members require recognition not just as workers, but as families, as mothers, and as young people with potential and dreams.

Impact on security and stability

Throughout 2009, migrants had lived with multiple levels of insecurity and instability.

They had to deal with job (and therefore livelihood) insecurities as a result of the global economic crisis, but also had to deal with the threats of mass deportations in February 2010, according to the Cabinet Resolution of 2008 on Migrant Workers, which allowed migrants to register for work for the final time in Thailand, with the final date being 28 February 2010. During 2009, levels of stress increased as migrants were pressured into entering a process to engage with the Burmese regime to have their nationality verified. As 2009 drew to a close, the tensions and hardships of the year bubbled near the surface. In December, 2,000 female migrant workers at the Top Form Brassiere factory in Mae Sot went on strike over an assault on two of the employees' relatives by four security officers. The workers' anger could not be quelled even by the show of armed force by the Thai authorities. Soldiers armed with rifles faced off the angry workers.[9] The workers demanded that the factory owner re-hire the workers who had been sacked and provide the welfare benefits they were due.

The future

Migrants from Burma/Myanmar have faced the economic downturn with resilience, but it is taking its toll, and situations like the one at the Top Form Brassiere factory may well flare up if migrants are further marginalized by the impact of the economic downturn and are excluded from recovery packages and from policy discussions which affect their lives.

The restrictions on migrants forming unions in Thailand has left migrants stranded in this time of economic crisis with few options available to ameliorate the situation. As a significant section of the labour force in Thailand, migrants must be able to have a voice and a standing to ensure that all work places provide decent work in Thailand.

Migrant workers are actively trying to improve their working conditions and to address the insecurity and exploitation they face. Migrant workers have formed their own labour associations, are educating themselves about Thai unions and discussing with union leaders the possibilities of joining Thai unions. They are co-ordinating with other sectors of the host population, a strategy that is particularly important for migrant women, who do well in leading and organizing workers informally, but who do not currently take the lead in more formal structures like associations. Migrant women have connected with Thai and regional women's movements to improve not only their working conditions, but also their safety and security in the household and in daily life and to strengthen their role as advocates for justice.

If migrants are ignored in these critical times, their social safety nets will continue to wear thin, and community structures may break down. Policies of exclusion, and tolerance of exploitation of certain sectors of society, harm the fabric of society, creating antagonism and anger. Therefore, the building of social cohesion and the integration of migrant workers and their families into Thai society is of particular importance now. Integration can be facilitated in the workplace, at educational facilities and in social and religious activities. Women migrant workers will be leading players, and are already leading the way with their connections of sisterhood and solidarity nationally and regionally.

Acknowledgements

MAP Foundation continues to work closely with the migrant communities and to document current situations. Our Women Exchange Program, supported by the Nobel Women's Initiative, is conducting workshops and focus group discussions with migrant and refugee women along the Thai-Burma border to develop a report on Discrimination Against Migrant Women. Soe Lin Aung, with institutional support from MAP Foundation, was awarded a grant from the Global Consortium on Security Transformation to develop a paper on 'Situating (in)security: Transforming security paradigms vis-à-vis migrant communities on the Thai-Burma border'.

Notes

1. In June 1989, the ruling military regime changed the name of the country from Burma to Myanmar. The UK, the USA and democracy activists continue to use the name Burma.
2. From the outcome document (p. 1) of the UN conference on the world financial and economic crisis and its impact on development, i.e. the UNGA Resolution adopted on 13 July 2009, numbered 63/303, www.un.org/ga/search/view_doc.asp?symbol=A/RES/63/303&Lang=E (last accessed 6 April 2010).
3. The term 'irregular or undocumented migrants' refers to people who migrate in search of employment in violation of laws and regulation governing migration. A much less acceptable term is 'illegal migrants', unacceptable because it suggests the migrant is illegal rather than that their actions are illegal.
4. Figures published by the Department of Employment, Ministry of Labour, reproduced on the MAP Foundation website, www.mapfoundationcm.org
5. The Ayeyawady-Chao Phraya-Mekong Economic Cooperation Strategy (ACMECS) is a co-operation framework amongst Cambodia, Lao PDR, Myanmar, Thailand and Vietnam to utilize member countries' diverse strengths and to promote development in the sub-region. Prime Minister Thaksin Shinawatra of Thailand initiated the establishment of this co-operation framework in April 2003.
6. Ministry of Labour analysis suggests that there were 300,000 children aged 15–17 years legally employed in registered establishments in 2005 (60 per cent male and 40 per cent female) (ILO, 2008; Seangpassa, 2009).
7. These workers later contacted MAP Foundation from Jordan when they were being threatened with deportation after arguments erupted between Burmese and Bangladeshi migrant workers. See also Pi Pi (2010).

8. Discussions in recent Women Exchange meetings. Also noted in Belton and Maung (2004).
9. Evidence from eye-witness accounts by MAP Foundation volunteers and a report in *The Nation* (2009).

Bibliography

Arnold, D. and Hewison, K. (2006) 'Exploitation in global supply chains: Burmese migrant workers in Mae Sot, Thailand', in K. Hewison and K. Young (eds), *Transnational Migrants and Work in Asia*, pp. 165–190, Routledge and City University of Hong Kong South East Asia.

Aung, K. and Aung, S.L. (2009) *Critical Times: Migrants and the Economy in Chiang Mai and Mae Sot*, MAP Foundation, Chiang Mai, Thailand.

Belton, S. and Maung, C. (2004) 'Fertility and abortion: Burmese women's health on the Thai-Burma border', *Forced Migration Review*, 19, pp. 36–37.

Government Public Relations Department (2009) *Special Economic Zone to be Established Along the Thai-Myanmar Border*, http://thailand.prd.go.th/view_inside.php?id=4464 (last accessed 30 July 2010).

Huguet, J.W. and Punpuing, S. (2005) *International Migration in Thailand*, International Organisation for Migration, Bangkok.

ILO (2008) *Overview of Child Labour in Thailand*, ILO, www.ilo.org/public/english///region/asro/bangkok/download/yr2008/cl08_overview.pdf (last accessed 18 November 2010).

Kusakabe, K. and Pearson, R. (2007) 'Policy contradictions and women migrant workers: a case study of Burmese women workers in Thailand's border factories', presented at the Workshop on Female Labor Migration in Globalizing Asia: Translocal/Transnational Identities and Agencies, 13–14 September 2007, National University of Singapore, Singapore.

Macan-Markar, M. (2003) 'Thailand's "cesspool" of worker abuse', *Asia Times*, www.atimes.com/atimes/Southeast_Asia/EJ03Ae01.html (last accessed 18 November 2010).

Macan-Markar, M. (2009) 'Economic crisis hits Myanmar's migrant women', *Asia Times*, www.atimes.com/atimes/Southeast_Asia/KI01Ae01.html (last accessed 18 November 2010).

MAP Foundation (2006) *No Human Being is Illegal 1996–2006: No Migrant Worker is Illegal*, MAP Foundation, www.mapfoundationcm.org/eng/PDF/eng/map10yrsbook.pdf (last accessed 18 November 2010).

Pi Pi, S. (2010) 'Burmese workers in Jordan involved in workplace altercation', *Mizzima*, www.mizzima.com/news/regional/3361-burmese-workers-in-jordan-involved-in-workplace-altercation.html (last accessed 13 May 2010).

Pongsawat, P. (2007) *Border Partial Citizenship, Border Towns, and Thai–Myanmar Cross-Border Development: Case Studies at the Thai Border Towns*, University of California at Berkeley, Department of City and Regional Planning, Berkeley, CA.

Sang Kook, L. (2007) *Integrating Others: A Study of Border Social System in the Thailand-Burma Borderland*, National University of Singapore, Department of Sociology, Singapore.

Seangpassa, C. (2009) 'Ministry wants to monitor Burmese migrant schools', *The Nation*, www.statelessperson.com/www/?q=node/6828 (last accessed 18 November 2010).

Somavia, J. (2008) Message by Juan Somavia, Director-General of the International Labour Office on the occasion of International Migrants Day, www.ilo.org/public/english/bureau/dgo/speeches/somavia/2008/migrants.pdf (last accessed 31 December 2009).

The Economist (2009) 'Myanmar's overflow: migrant workers battered by the slump'.

The Nation (2009) 'Some 2,000 Burmese workers protest inside bra factory in Tak', www.nationmultimedia.com/home/Some-2000-Burmese-workers-at-bra-plant-end-strike-30118859.html (last accessed 13 May 2010).

Tsuneishi, T. (2007) 'Thailand's economic cooperation with neighboring countries and its effects on economic development within Thailand', IDE Discussion Paper no. 115.

UNDP (2009) 'Overcoming barriers: human mobility and development', Human Development Report, UNDP.

UN–INSTRAW (2007) 'The feminization of international labour migration', Working Paper 1, Santo Domingo, Dominican Republic: UN–INSTRAW.

World Bank (2006) 'Labour migration in the Greater Mekong Subregion', Synthesis Report: Phase 1, World Bank, http://siteresources.worldbank.org/INTTHAILAND/Resources/333200-1089943634036/475256-1151398858396/LM_in_GMSs_Nov06.pdf (last accessed 18 November 2010).

About the authors

Jackie Pollock is Executive Director of MAP Foundation (Migrant Assistance Programme), Thailand.

Soe Lin Aung is a Research Officer at MAP Foundation.

CHAPTER 5

Feminized recession: impact of the global financial crisis on women garment workers in the Philippines

Kristina Gaerlan, Marion Cabrera, Patricia Samia and Ed L. Santoalla

This chapter first appeared in *Gender & Development* 18(2), pp. 229–240, July 2010.

This chapter discusses the findings of Oxfam-commissioned research into the impact of the economic crisis on women garment workers in the Philippines. It provides policy recommendations aiming to ensure that measures put in place by the government and international bodies support the women workers who have seen their jobs lost or their working conditions worsen, and ensure that recovery measures support the goal of gender equality rather than working against this.

Introduction

Financial crises are nothing new in South-East Asia. The region was celebrated during the early part of the 1990s for its 'tiger economies', and was one of the main magnets of portfolio investments – often referred to as 'hot money' – flowing in from the developed nations of the West. The countries of the region were among the first to fall into the Asian economic crisis of 1997. The crisis began in Thailand, when portfolio investors withdrew their funds at the first signs of a property bubble bursting in that country. The lessons learned by South-East Asian economies since then are said to have made them stronger – enough for them to withstand the initial effects of the still unfolding global financial meltdown that originated in the USA last year.

A case in point is the Philippines, whose government, early on in the current crisis, has stated that financial and banking reforms instituted since 1997 have offered a bit of protection from the US sub-prime fallout. This, however, is not to say that the Philippines is totally insulated; the highly publicized closure of big companies making products for major US and European industries early this year has already provided a foretaste of things to come.

According to the Semiconductor and Electronics Industries in the Philippines, Inc. (SEIPI), the industry suffered an 8 per cent decline in 2008. It will remain in the red until end 2009, largely due to the effects of the global financial crisis. Worldwide, revenues of the semiconductor industry in 2009 are estimated to reach only US$198 billion, as against US$255 billion in 2008 (Semiconductor Industry Association, 2009).

Textile and garments are the country's second largest export industry after the chip and electronics makers, employing an estimated workforce of 150,000. However, the industry has long been edged out by lower-cost producers in China, Indonesia, Vietnam, India, Morocco, and Turkey. The crisis has made companies in the US and Europe even more cost-conscious, especially in terms of labour costs vis-à-vis productivity.

This research was conducted to find out the specific impact of the global economic crisis on Filipino women workers. It is part of a study being conducted by Oxfam GB in East Asia on the impact of the economic crisis on women in five countries of the Association of Southeast Asian Nations (ASEAN): Vietnam, Cambodia, Philippines, Indonesia, and Thailand. This research was conducted in the context of the hypothesis that Filipino women are more vulnerable to the impact of the crisis than men in the same social and economic groups, and hence they have been disproportionately affected by the crisis.

The research context

The geographical focus of this study is the Calabarzon area, where many crisis-triggered company closures, retrenchments, and lay-offs have been occurring. The Philippine Senate, citing projections by the labour group Pagkakaisa ng Manggagawa sa Timog Katagalugan-Kilusang Mayo Uno (Union of Workers in Southern Tagalog May 1 Movement), has said that more than 40,000 workers in the Calabarzon area are set to lose their jobs by the first half of the present year. Of these, they estimate that 35,000 will be from electronics and automotive parts factories inside the Laguna Technopark.

This crisis comes on top of a pre-existing high level of unemployment. The highest unemployment rate among women was reported in the National Capital Region, where 11.7 per cent of the region's labour force is unemployed. Calabarzon and Central Luzon follow with 9.0 per cent and is the second largest contributor to total unemployed women in the Philippines with 18.7 per cent, with the National Capital Region (Metro Manila) coming in first with 24.8 per cent (National Statistics Office Gender and Development Committee, 2009).

There are no available gender-disaggregated data on local retrenchments and lay-offs that have occurred since the onset of the global financial crisis. It is safe to say, however, that formally employed women in the electronics, semi-conductors, telecommunications, and garments industries, as well as the other industries engaged in production for export, have been the hardest hit by the crisis. As also pointed out earlier, women comprise the majority of workforces in these largely export-oriented industries.

Research objectives and methodology

The research was conducted for the purpose of:

- assessing the impact of the financial crisis on women in the Philippines;
- analysing the gendered nature of government responses to the crisis and their impact on women workers so far; and
- developing a set of recommendations for consideration by the Philippine government and by regional institutions and donors.

The study covered women workers in both the formal and the informal economies. We focused on women in several industries: cable television and telecommunications, garments, semiconductors, and electronics. These are industries that employ women workers and thus have women in the majority of the workforce that have been retrenched or laid off due to crisis-triggered company closures. The study also looked into the situation of women in the informal sector, as represented by mothers engaged in the manufacture of rags, socks, and other items made from scrap textiles.

The authors conducted three focus-group discussions (FGDs), involving a total of 28 participants ranging in age from 18 to 70. Of these, 18 were women. The first FGD was held in Mandaluyong City, with retrenched workers from the cable television, telecommunications, and semiconductor industries. The second was held with retrenched workers from various companies located in the Cavite Export Processing Zone found in the coastal town of Rosario, Cavite. The participants came mostly from the semiconductors and garments industries. The third group consisted of home-based workers making rags and socks in the Metro Manila town of Pateros and city of Taguig.

From the focus groups, the authors identified two participants and invited them to more intimate, one-to-one conversations, so that their stories could be used as case studies. In addition, two key informants were interviewed as well. The first was an officer of the Business Processing Association of the Philippines, who spoke at length on industry's defiance of recessionary trends, as well as growth prospects. The second key informant was the corporate affairs manager of Intel Philippines Corporation, which had been the first big company to announce that it was ceasing operations in the Philippines, in the wake of the global financial crisis. The Intel representative discussed the comprehensive retrenchment and closure plan to be followed by the management team.

Because there are no large disparities in the trends and practices of the affected industries across regions, the women's stories provided a comprehensive picture of the impact of the crisis on low- and middle-income Filipino women as a whole.

Findings

Continuing job insecurity through 'casualization'

FGD participants from special economic zones or export processing zones said that job losses were frequent and regular, and entirely independent of economic recession. Often, job losses occurred as soon as employees' six-month probation contracts were finished. Women would prepare for this by searching for jobs with other companies based within the export-processing zone. Each time, this process would entail yet another round of police and security clearances as well as fit-to-work medical check-ups, easily costing the individual at least US$44. Months would be spent processing and following up applications. After being hired, the worker would have to go through the same cycle again when the next six-month contract had run its course.

Heightened poverty and hunger

The loss of their jobs owing to retrenchment and lay-offs had clearly pushed women workers of crisis-affected companies deeper into poverty. This was especially true for FGD participants from the garments sector, where it has been estimated that 90 per cent of those holding new jobs that are under threat of disappearing because of the crisis are women living in poverty (Van der Gaag, 2009).

The clearest expression of poverty is the inability of large numbers of Filipinos to meet the most basic of needs for subsistence. Traditionally, food is the biggest expense of the poor Filipino household. Over the years, food accounted for almost 60 per cent of expenses by the bottom 30 per cent of the income group. But the focus group participants' experience showed that job loss, coupled with the steady rise in prices of basic commodities, has downgraded food consumption in terms of both quantity and quality. National Statistical Coordination Board (NSCB) data in 2003 showed that more than 11 million Filipinos were considered food-poor or living below subsistence level. The Food and Agricultural Organisation reported in 2005 that there were more than 17 million undernourished Filipinos.

One woman participant told us that the price of canned milk (as distinct from infant formula milk) that she was using to feed her baby had doubled. This was the same woman that, with her eyes welling up, admitted that she and her husband skipped meals to ensure the baby had milk. '*Sumasala din*', she said, referring to how the couple has had to forgo some meals. As a people, Filipinos are known for their fondness for eating, evident in the numerous food stands, establishments and vendors at any given time in any given place. In between the three main meals are the midday and afternoon snacks. Religious rituals, community festivities and family gatherings are planned around the food to be served and shared within the occasion. Loosely translated, the word '*sumasala*' means 'to lapse'. The use of the word '*sumasala*' to refer to being forced to skip a meal thus suggests an unacceptable lapse or default.

A second participant said that after her daughter had been laid off from work, she had not been able to find the money to feed her child. The participant had found a solution: she fed the child a chocolate-flavoured drink rather than the usual canned milk. This chocolate powder drink came in single-serve packs and was more affordable than the milk. Another said she sometimes needed to sacrifice midday and mid-afternoon snacks, so that the money could be used instead for the children's transportation to school. One home-based woman worker said her household has not given up snacks, but these had become no more than one piece of *pan de sal* with a cup of coffee.

Another said she now uses a different variety of rice as a cost-cutting measure, whereas she used to buy government-procured rice. One elderly participant said: 'Sometimes, we don't buy rice anymore, we depend on the free rice distributed to the Grade One students in public schools'.

Lifestyle changes: letting go of non-essentials

Another specific effect of the global financial crisis on women workers that surfaced during the FGDs was the reduction of spending on leisure and recreation. A male participant said: 'Before, I could give my wife a weekly shopping allowance. Without fail, she would be at the mall every weekend. But it's been two years now since we last entered a mall'. For the lower-income households, one of the most obvious effects of the crisis was giving up the fast-food meals, the equivalent of 'splurging' when there is extra money.

One participant described the middle-class 'belt-tightening' of foregoing a spa or hair treatment, or a new piece of clothing. 'My lifestyle really changed. In the past, every month, I would be at the salon. I could afford to take care of myself', one participant said.

In terms of other expenses, many participants also experienced interruptions in their electricity supply, due to failure to settle their bills promptly. The monthly electricity bill occupied the number two slot in the majority of the participants' lists of important expenditure, next to food. This was consistent with the findings of the 2006 Family Income and Expenditure Survey of fuel, light, and water as among the household's highest expenses at 6 per cent to 7 per cent of total income.

Asked by the profile sheet to rank the other household expenses by importance, most ticked off food and education (the transportation fare and recess money of the children), and left items such as health and medicines as blank, belying the Filipinos' common disregard for health care as a concern and an investment. It should be noted, moreover, that basic education is free. For 72 per cent of poor households, the highest educational attainment was primary school education, which explains the minimal spending on education (Philippine Children's Foundation, 2005).

The implication of this insight from the FGDs is that spending on health care is a low priority among poor Filipino households. This, however, does not diminish the fact that poor Filipinos still spend more on health for the simple reason that government is not able to do so much for them in this regard. By government's own admission, its target to depend less on out-of-pocket payments and provide more social health insurance is still far from being realized as the share of out-of-pocket payments even increased to 49 per cent while the share of social insurance payments increased only slightly to 11 per cent in 2005. Based on the Health Sector Reform Agenda (HSRA), the target for out-of-pocket expenses is 20 per cent while the target for social insurance is 30 per cent. Meanwhile, the share of government on health expenditure declined to 29 per cent, which is also below the HSRA target of 40 per cent (NSCB, 2005).

Resilience and creativity built by old and new poverty

It has been said that the Asian financial crisis of 1997 prepared Filipinos for the global financial crisis of 2007. Despite the difficulties making up the everyday reality facing Filipinos, their resilience is notable and fascinating. This is often expressed in an inimitable brand of humour, which can make light of the most serious problems of daily survival. This Filipino grit can be explained by their phenomenal success in evolving strategies to cushion the blow of poverty, the form of second jobs, or 'sidelines' – alternative income sources to bridge the family from one day to the next.

Paguntalan (2002) often mentioned the term *diskarte*. This is often used in a number of contexts, including courtship, negotiation, and lastly, work. The word speaks of a woman's ability to transcend a situation or limitation. Women describe this as the attempt to solve the problems or courage in dealing with the problems encountered. The context within which women speak of *diskarte* ranges from being able to survive (*makaraos*) to transcendence (*malagpasan ang pagsubok*). *Diskarte* also employs certain strategies such as *lakas ng loob* (guts) and *kusang-loob* (initiative). *Diskarte* is very much evident in the stories of the women who participated in the FGDs.

1. *The informal economy as refuge.* The informal economy makes available these other means of earning a living. Women's ingenuity in balancing the household budget against expenses is best seen in the solutions found by the home-based workers of Rizal. One home-based worker said: 'I keep a small retail store. I also do the laundry, which means an extra $5.62. I'm also a trimmer, though the earnings from this are paltry, only 10 centavos or 0.002 US cents per rag'.

   Her companion, on the other hand, said that she uses a sewing machine for occasional dress repair and alteration jobs when it is not being used in the fabrication of rags and foot socks. However, the machine is best optimized in the run-up to the town fiesta, when neighbours want new curtains and cushion and bed covers. Another member of this group said she works three half-days a week as a janitor at a privately run nursery school: 'I clean the classrooms of a private school, for which I earn only monthly. But the work is only for half the day', she said.

Another strategy is to find sources of credit. Standard practice among the poor, particularly those who are engaged either as workers or entre-preneurs in the informal economy, is to rely on informal lenders. There are ethnic Filipinos who are into this type of business, but the iconic image of the moneylender in our cultural context is that of the 'Bombay', the local name for persons of South Asian (Indian) descent, who come to the Philippines and engage in a money-lending practice called '5–6'. Under this practice, one borrows Php5 and pays the lender back Php6, which represents an interest rate of 20 per cent per quarter, or 80 per cent per annum, as against the average bank rate of 4 per cent per quarter, or 16 per cent per annum. This is the most common form of usury practised in the Philippines and in the main it is the poor who are the victims, because 5–6 is the only credit resource available to them in the informal economy. You can see the 'Bombays' doing the rounds of wet markets[1] and neighbourhood *sari-sari* (variety) stores every day, collecting pay-ments from their clients.

As for savings, we found during the research that to pose a question on this subject, particularly in a time of crisis when people are jobless, and have nothing in their pockets, the sarcastic response that one tends to receive is: 'what savings are you talking about?'.

2. *Using the support system of family and friends.* Although almost perma-nent, the poverty of many Filipinos goes through ebbs and flows, peaks and troughs. As the Asian Development Bank (ADB) puts it, poverty in the Philippines is a dynamic phenomenon, where people move in and out of poverty over time. A first attempt to gauge chronic and tran-sient poverty found that, over a three-year period, about one-fifth of the surveyed households were chronically poor, whereas nearly one-third shifted into and out of poverty during the period. Almost always, how-ever, it is up to the woman to ensure that there is food on the table and that the most immediate needs of the household – water and health care – are met. For this, she has come up with ingenious ways of finding money (Schelzig, 2005).

The role of the extended Filipino family as a source of economic secu-rity, especially for poor families, and most especially in hard times, was clear in our research. In the focus groups, several participants had moved back in with their parents or parents-in-law, to save on rental in the face of job retrenchment.

Although one worker laid off from her job in a garments factory in the Cavite Export Processing Zone still had the husband's income to depend on for the family's sustenance, the loss of one income meant the family needed to move in with their parents as a temporary cost-saving solution. When one middle-class respondent was laid off, she was compelled to give up her flat, for which she was paying $202 in rent, and together with her son, transfer to her brother's house. Housing typically represents the second largest expense in the family budget, ranging from 8.8 per cent in 2003 to 9 per cent in the latest 2006 income and expenditure survey. Thus, any savings on the monthly rental considerably eases up the burden brought about by the crisis.

One participant was already one year behind in paying the rent on his apartment, but he chose not to be weighed down by this problem. For one, he explained, the landlady seemed to understand as it appeared that several of his co-tenants in a 12-door apartment row were also on rental arrears. Beyond that, however, the landlady seemed to understand their plight and all she was asking of her tenants was that they settle their light bills promptly, so that the meter would not be removed by the power company.

Not surprisingly, the participants who owned, and not rented, their houses were faring better in making the household budget suffice, despite the income squeeze across the board. These homeowners, who tended to be among the older respondents with ages ranging from 50 to 60, spoke of their difficulties, on the other hand, of earning for an entire household of children and grandchildren. Even though they were past their reproductive years, they looked at the burden of providing for the multiple-family household as primarily their own. 'What can you do?' one of the women asked, 'You cannot turn them out'.

One participant narrated how everyone in the household was contributing to meeting the expenses:

> My daughter [whose family lives with her] also helps in preparing the materials and assembling the parts of a rag. The pay that she gets is what we spend on food as she and her husband stay with me.

One woman trapped in the 'casualization' cycle at the export processing zone relied on a distant relative for loans for her daily subsistence when she was out of work: 'I just keep on borrowing money and when I'm able to find work, that's when I pay'.

These stories of family solidarity in hard times challenge the value modern society has come to assign to the Western requisites of financial independence and physical space by the age of 18.

Discussion

The results of this study validate the premises by which it was conducted, to wit:

- that women are over-represented in sectors where the crisis has caused huge job cuts (e.g. export manufacturing, garments industry, electronics, and services);
- that women tend to be employed in precarious jobs where they are more likely to be fired first or experience aggravated working conditions (e.g. as migrant workers and in the garments industry); and
- that women tend to be responsible for family welfare, and so will be adversely affected by cuts in public spending on safety nets and reduction in remittance income.

The crisis, though, is testifying once again to the ability of Filipino women to come up with creative and ingenious ways of coping and surviving. The informal economy continues to provide women with alternative platforms for income generation and/or supplementation, and the extended family (consistent with Filipino norms and values), remains a reliable source of psycho-social and material support during times of crises. Such refuge and support, however, cannot be enough.

Recommendations

The first set of recommendations that we advanced to policymakers in the wake of our research were as follows. The first set focus on advocacy for sustainable macroeconomic development.

- To develop and implement the bailout plan being proposed by economists and labour groups that will put money into the hands of retrenched, laid off, and otherwise jobless workers to allow them to address immediate family and economic needs;
- to spur agricultural development to create jobs in the countryside;
- to push for macroeconomic policy that enables the country not only to compete effectively in the world market, but more importantly, to provide first for the needs of its own people. The policy should stipulate the maintenance of public budgets for social spending to ensure employment security, universal income, public health and education, and housing, particularly during emergencies arising from developments such as the global financial crisis;
- to revive/re-intensify the freedom from debt campaign, specifically, call for suspension of the payment of public debt in order for resources earmarked for the servicing of such debt to be used instead in funding national efforts to recover from the effects of the global financial crisis. This may also be an opportune time – given the 'double whammy' of the financial and climate change crises (which is putting financial investments by developed countries in developing ones) – to renegotiate the terms of payment for such debt away from structural impositions by multilaterals such as the International Monetary Fund–World Bank and

ADB that have, in the first place, made the country export-oriented and vulnerable to international economic shocks.

The second set of recommendations from our research concern advocacy for the protection of workers' rights, particularly women employed in export industries, in foreign markets, and in the informal economy. We need to ensure that the following is achieved:

- Protection of the rights of migrant workers in the event of job losses, ensuring their safe return to, and reintegration in, their home countries. For those who cannot return, there should be no forced return, their security should be guaranteed, and they should be provided with employment and a basic minimum income.
- Protection of women workers in particular from vulnerabilities they continue to be exposed to in the globalized working environment, including economic and human rights abuses committed in foreign labour markets where they are employed mostly as domestic helpers; protect women workers from casualization, reduced working hours, and flexible working arrangements that companies are implementing to cope with the financial crisis' impact on the local economy. For social protection of women, additional provisioning must be done to provide livelihood and training, especially to those situated in difficult circumstances, such as loss of jobs in the face of the global financial crisis.
- Review of government programmes that train Overseas Filipino Workers (OFWs) and members of their families in finance and business management skills to prepare them for re-entry into the mainstream national economy at the end of their work contracts. Details of such training programmes should be published so that returning OFWs, many of whom come from the provinces will know about and will be able to access them.
- Review of the Overseas Workers' Welfare Fund, which was established from proceeds of OFW contributions, to provide financial and material support for whenever members or their dependents are in need, such as during times of emergencies or to pay off debts incurred by OFWs during their search for job placements. The Fund should include components specifically addressing the needs of women OFWs not only as breadwinners, but also as important economic actors in context, particularly of the fact that they are fast becoming a major source of dollar earnings for the national economy.
- Review of the Philippine Labor Code – already weak in the first place owing to provisions that allow contractualization, violations of minimum wage and labour standards (including proper wage, leaves, and social insurance benefits) in the guise of cost-cutting and cost management, and worst, violations of the human rights of protesting workers – is also in order to put a stop to new potentially anti-labour practices that

have arisen under conditions of globalization and the global financial crisis.

- Institutionalization of standards for the valuation of women's labour (home-based/home-bound) and other workers in the informal economy through the enactment of the proposed Magna Carta of Workers in the Informal Economy.
- Active engagement in the process of formulating the implementing rules and regulations (IRR) of the recently enacted Philippine Magna Carta of Women to ensure inclusion of the provisions mandating protection of the political, economic, human, and gender rights of women, particularly those in the workplace.

Conclusion

There is a need for policy changes to make existing poverty-mitigation pro-grammes more effective. There is also a need to address squarely the issue of casualization and other abuses of workers' economic and political rights that are being perpetrated and tolerated in the name of business survival. This has placed Filipino workers in general and women workers in particular in a state of indignity and insecurity that, in a way, could also be interpreted, albeit negatively, as a source of their 'resilience'; that is, becoming used to constant difficulties and coasting along without complaining until the next job open-ing and until the loans fall due, and recourse to desperate and risky measures becomes inevitable.

Acknowledgements

This article is based on research conducted for Oxfam GB Philippines by Kristina Gaerlan (team leader), Marion Cabrera and Patricia Samia, and edited by Ed L. Santoalla, economic justice policy analyst and research manager, Oxfam GB, Philippines.

Note

1. 'Wet markets' are where informal vendors sell fresh meat, fish and other farm produce. Compared with supermarkets or groceries, wet markets don't have refrigeration, and vendors rely on blocks of ice to keep their goods from spoiling. This keeps the pavilions in which vendor stalls are situated in a state of constant 'wetness', hence the term.

References

National Statistics Office Gender and Development Committee (2009) 'Unemployed women', Gender factsheet, http://www.census.gov.ph/data/specialevents/cedaw2009/factsheets/unemployed.pdf (last accessed 11 May 2010).

NSCB (2005) 'Government expenditure on health', Philippine National Health Accounts, http://www.nscb.gov.ph/stats/pnha/2005/government.asp (last accessed 13 July 2009).

Paguntalan, A.M. (2002) *Nimble Fingers, Clenched Fists: Dynamics of Structure, Agency and Women's Spaces in a Manufacturing Company*, University of the Philippines Center for Women's Studies and The Ford Foundation, http://cws.upd.edu.ph/index.php?name=Sections&req=viewarticle&artid=22&allpages=1&theme=Printer (last accessed 11 August 2009).

Philippine Children's Foundation (2005) *Poor Education*, www.philippine childrensfoundation.org/pooreducation.shtml (last accessed 11 July 2009).

Schelzig, K. (2005) *Poverty in the Philippines: Income, Assets and Access*, Asian Development Bank, http://www.adb.org/Documents/Books/Poverty-in-the-Philippines/Poverty-in-the-Philippines.pdf (last accessed 11 July 2009).

Semiconductor Industry Association (2009) 'Global semiconductor sales fell by 2.8 percent in 2008', http://www.sia-online.org/cs/papers_publications/press_release_detail?pressrelease.id=1534 (last accessed 31 July 2009).

Van der Gaag, N. (2009) 'The impact of the global financial crisis on girls and young women', March 2009, http://www.devstud.org.uk/downloads/4a1512f025f74_GenderSG_vanderGaag_fincris_youngwomen.pdf (last accessed 18 November 2010).

About the authors

Kristina N. Gaerlan, Research Team Leader, has been active in social development advocacy work since the 1980s and in feminist research since the 1990s.

Marion Bernadette G. Cabrera is Programme Coordinator for governance, communications, and democracy for Isis International.

Patricia Morales-Samia, is an independent consultant specializing in social enterprise development and project development.

Ed Santoalla, project manager and editor, is Policy Analyst and Research Manager for the Economic Justice Programme of Oxfam in the Philippines.

CHAPTER 6

Securing the fruits of their labours: the effect of the crisis on women farm workers in Peru's Ica valley

Reineira Arguello

This chapter first appeared in *Gender & Development* 18(2), pp. 241–247, July 2010.

Despite immediate promises of economic recovery by some Latin American gov-ernments, women in some regions of the continent are feeling the aftermath of the crisis deeply. This is because of both the interconnectedness of their regions to the export market, and pre-existing economic policies and social factors, includ-ing gender inequality that strengthens inequalities. These factors are intensifying the impact of the crisis on women's lives. This chapter draws on Womankind Worldwide research into the case of women farm workers in Peru's Ica valley. It discusses how the economic crisis is increasing women's unemployment, and worsening women's poverty. An analysis of the role of a women's rights organiza-tion in responding to the crisis reveals that solutions to the problems brought by the crisis must go beyond macroeconomic responses.

Introduction

For Latin American countries, the effects of the economic crisis in the global North have been mainly felt in three areas: trade, remittances, and financial credit (Winograd and Molina, 2009). However, the crisis has affected countries in the Latin American continent to different degrees, and in different ways. Previous economic measures, involving accumulating mechanisms for a 'rainy day', have allowed countries such as Chile to achieve some economic growth, despite the crisis (ibid.). Brazil, which launched the 'PAC' (Accelerated Growth Programme), has managed to come out quite well from the global financial crisis.[1] However, other Latin American countries are not in the same position, and the crisis aftermath is seriously affecting the lives of inhabitants of regions and localities, in particular in countries that are heavily dependent on export-oriented markets.

In the case of Peru, spokespeople for the government initially denied that the effects of the crisis could reach the country: Alan Garcia's defiant declarations to the media suggested that Peru had especial protection from the crisis.[2] However, for around 100,000 women who work in agribusiness (Maranon and Moreyra, 2009), and represent two thirds of the workforce of that sector, it did not take long to realize that for them, the effects of the crisis were not a remote threat. Employers in the Peruvian regions of La Libertad and Ica (respectively, homes to 52 per cent and 42 per cent of the agribusiness production in the country)[3] have blamed the crisis as a reason for cancelling many job contracts. Our research, on which this chapter is based, showed that many workers who have retained their jobs have experienced a significant reduction in wages, and some have been forced to work longer hours without additional pay.

Although men and women have both been affected by the crisis, this article primarily focuses on the effect of the crisis on women's employment in agribusiness. It shows how pre-existing gender inequalities have worsened women's situation in the labour market during the crisis. Households that are solely, or mainly, dependent on women's wages are more likely to have been economically poor to start with. Women and their dependents are, therefore, likely to experience unemployment as a disaster which plunges them into very harsh living conditions, and may cause them to cross the line into acute poverty.

Gender-sensitive policies to enable communities and households to survive are urgently required. The state cannot and should not confine its role to designing (apparently gender-neutral) macroeconomic measures. It needs to create an enabling environment for women in particular, to enable them to meet their gender-specific needs and enable them to support the families who depend on their income, by evolving policies that will help families survive the crisis. An understanding of the survival strategies of families and households, where the needs of women are often missed or misunderstood by policymakers, is vital to tackling endemic inequalities that maintain women in a structurally disadvantaged position, and places the bitterest burden of the crisis on women and their dependents.

This article draws on the experience of The Women's Federation of Ica (FEPROMU), a non-government organization that has worked with women who endured different forms of violence since 1994. FEPROMU is currently working with Womankind Worldwide (www.womankind.org), a UK-based international development organization. Womankind Worldwide works in partnership in Peru with FEPROMU and other women's rights organizations, such as the Association Aurora Vivar, on different projects to eliminate violence against women, and increase women's civil and political participation. Womankind Worldwide works with its partners to support women in Peru to have a voice in important government reforms that may offer women equal grounds to fight discrimination and exclusion. Womankind Worldwide is also currently working with FEPROMU on a project on sexual and reproductive rights for adolescents in the region, many of which are siblings of women who work in agro-industry.

In 2009, FEPROMU decided to systematically collect testimonies of women workers affected by the crisis. The research included in-depth interviews, focus groups, testimonies and structured interviews, and focused on women workers in agro-industry and their dependants.

The crisis and its impact on women workers in Ica

The labour of women workers in the Ica valley has contributed to the boom of agribusiness in Peru – which was worth US$1,500 million in 2007, nearly double that from 2004. Many agricultural products, including asparagus, oranges, paprika, lemon, avocadoes and grapes (including the famous Peruvian Pisco) are grown in Ica by women farm-hands. The agricultural production from Ica represents 42 per cent of the total agricultural exports from the country. In 2009, Peru faced a 16 per cent reduction in exports of agricultural products, which according to the Ministry of Agriculture was because of the economic stagnation of Peru's primary trade partners, the USA and the EU. This reduction represented a drop of 30 per cent in the demand for labour in the agribusiness sector.[4]

It is clear that in the Ica region, the crisis has impacted negatively on women's lives, increasing levels of vulnerability, marginalization and poverty. However, a pervasive environment of discrimination, together with ingrained labour rights violations and gender inequalities, means that focusing attention solely on the impact of the crisis hides the persistent dynamics of exploitation that weaken women's position in the labour market.

Women in Peru make up a large percentage of workers in the production of agricultural export, where the crisis has been felt most strongly. This has deeply affected women in the sector, where agribusiness employers have reduced labour costs and ignored rules on reasonable female employment, adequate salaries and the freedom to unionize. In 2000, the Peruvian parliament passed the Law that Approves the Norms for the Promotion of the Agrarian Sector (Law 27360), which lessened protection for the rights of workers in this sector. The crisis has worsened the already harsh labour conditions.

Women workers who were about to gain permanent positions after five years of work have been laid off, and employers have justified this by saying it is a result of the crisis. A 25-year-old worker who has been living in Ica for nearly four years, and is the single mother of two children, told us:

> They fired me arguing that the demand on the product is very low; this is not true as they are hiring new people. I have been working for nearly four years in this company and they are just firing old employees ... I do not know what to do with my two children on my own.[5]

This speaker's children had been previously attending in a nursery opened by FEPROMU to help the children of women who work in agro-industry.

Some seasonal workers we spoke to had had their contracts cancelled before the end. Workers also report increased levels of sexual harassment towards women, who work in farms which are mainly supervised by men; this is because women are unable to argue owing to increased desperation to keep their jobs:

> ... supervisors felt they have the right to touch us; they do it knowing that we cannot complain because we need the job to feed our families.[6]

FEPROMU's research revealed that women who lose their jobs are adopting survival dynamics, where new roles and responsibilities are given to family members. Looking for work in other areas of the informal sector becomes a task for women heads of the household; eldest boys and girls are forced to migrate to cities such as Lima, searching for work and exposing them to abuse and exploitation; younger girl members of the family have to take care of the household in the absence of the mother, which results in falling school attendance. Ana, aged 13, was part of FEPROMU'S project with adolescents, working as a social promoter. She said: 'I have to leave the project work, I cannot be a promoter any longer, as I have to look after my mum, by looking for a job ...'[7]

Furthermore, in recent months an increase in the number of girls trafficked and in prostitution has been noticed by FEPROMU in the area of Ica.

Even if women have been able to keep their jobs, the crisis has weakened their bargaining position with employers. In a region where 40 per cent of people live under the poverty threshold (according to the 2005 census), even before the crisis, there was no shortage of women desperate to find work. Labour in the agribusiness sector is made up primarily of temporary workers – the vast majority of whom are women – who only obtain permanent contracts after five years of continuous work in the farm (Centro Peruano de Estudios Sociales, 2009). Young women from all over Peru have been attracted to Ica by the promise of steady work and decent wages. Most of them have been brought by *enganchadores* ('catchers'), who, for a percentage pay by the companies, travel to faraway areas in Peru located mainly in the Andes, promising women, often with children, a new life through a job that will drive them to the larger farms across the region.

Research respondents pointed out that once in Ica, migrant workers find living conditions very difficult. Commonly, the new arrivals have built improvised huts owned by the company, which typically lack running water, electricity and sanitation. These housing conditions are similar to many of the families already living in Ica, who lost their homes in an earthquake in 2007, and are still living in huts made of cardboard and wood, or tents donated by international aid agencies. FEPROMU has visited the places where women live; interviews of women give accounts of similar living conditions for most of the workers in the agribusiness sector in the region of Ica.

According to information collected from women workers by FEPROMU, the work itself was punishing, even before the crisis. For the majority of these women, the day started around 03:00, when they did the housework and cooked, before a two-hour ride to the farms. Some women said that they had to stand or crouch all day picking, while others were continuously exposed to toxic pesticides. Most of these women had children; it is common to have children young, and teen pregnancy is widespread. Children often stayed in the hut while their mothers were working, and were looked after by brothers and sisters who were often just a few years older. These children tended to be malnourished and this, along with the lack of basic sanitation, made them prone to diseases, some of which may prevent them from developing normally.

It was common before the crisis for both male and female workers to be expected to work over 12 hours per day (instead of the legal 8 working hours), without being paid any overtime. In some cases, workers reported being forced to do piecework – for instance, they will be told to pick a number of vines, regardless of how long it may take them to do so. Health and safety is a further area of concern. Transport conditions are cramped, with workers frequently piled up in small lorries and vans with little or no concern for their safety. The physical demands of the job also pose a threat to the health and physical integrity of workers, and legal regulations in this respect are routinely overlooked.

In our research we found that since the economic crisis took hold, women workers have been forced to work longer hours without extra pay, and they have consequently had less time to rest and complete extra activities in the household. This results in less time to take care of other members of the household, including preparing food and other essential caring activities. This makes everyone more vulnerable to ill-health and disease, and diminishes their ability to cope. Carmen, aged 21, told FEPROMU:

> Every day my quota of asparagus to pick is increased by my supervisor. I have to work longer hours to finish it otherwise they won't pay me. I am tired and I feel depressed. I can no longer cook or look after my children after work. I work more than 11 hours a day, but I cannot complain.[8]

FEPROMU's response to the crisis

While the Peruvian state focuses on both development of macroeconomic policies and economic packages that maintain competitiveness in the agribusiness sector as a way to reduce the impact of the crisis, FEPROMU is advocating for a social protection policy that is able to tackle women's growing poverty.

Womankind and FEPROMU believe that structures and practices that enforce poverty and discrimination against women diminish women's likelihood of attaining coping strategies that allow a decent recovery from shocks such as the loss of income caused by the crisis. Women's denial of basic human rights in the workplace, such as freedom of association and bargaining power, condemns women to endemic poverty and marginalization and enables their exploitation and exclusion.

At the local level, FEPROMU has identified how women's vulnerability has increased and some elements of the crisis' aftermath for women and their families, and is trying to prevent and address the different dimensions of the crisis in the lives of the poor women and men. At the regional level, FEPROMU is engaged in an ongoing struggle for a government review on the gender impact of the crisis and gender policies. They believe that an understanding of household dynamics, and how these are being affected in crisis time, is needed in order to inform the government on effective service provision that tackles different dimensions of the crisis' aftermath among household members.

FEPROMU is working continuously with women farm workers, informing and supporting them to organize and defend their rights. Lobbying the government to ensure that regular and reliable inspections in farming areas take place is, according to FEPROMU, a way to tackle the often reckless attitude of agribusiness owners towards enforcing labour rights that are enshrined in Peruvian legislation. Although the crisis has exposed some the effects of the loss of income on women in the supply side of the export market, other dynamics that maintain women in poverty and subordination should be challenged, in order to prevent a more severe feminization of poverty. This has been highlighted in the advocacy campaign of this organization, which believes that women workers' rights, and workers' rights in general, are fundamental to the ability of women to develop coping strategies in the crisis and should be part of a global policy response from states at national and international level that benefit from these women's labour.

Womankind Worldwide and FEPROMU have collaborated on offering women training in leadership and support to increase self-esteem and confidence to women who work in the agribusiness sector, and has contributed to the formation of unions that advocate the improvement of women workers' conditions and rights in the areas of Ica, La Libertad, Cajamarca, Amazonas and San Martin.

Womankind Worldwide believes that that the impact of the crisis is more acute for women owing to historical conditions that deepen women's poverty and marginalization. Although in the case of Peru it is clear that the immediate impact of the crisis is on women who are part of the export market, there are other silent effects of the crisis that need to be understood by governments in order to offer adequate social protection to meet women's needs. Childcare assistance and specific protection to pregnant women and to women heads of households should be offered to reduce the impact of the crisis on women and families.

We consider that it is fundamental that governments promote women's participation in the labour market through a framework that protects women from further exploitation. Therefore, Womankind Worldwide is calling on all governments to create enforcement mechanisms that enable the implementation of the notion of decent work, which allows for women in the formal economy and unregulated wageworkers, the self-employed and home workers, to enjoy safety at work and healthy working conditions.

Acknowledgements

The author thanks FEPROMU for all the inspirational work they do and the information and support to draft this article, and thanks as well Susana Klien, Womankind Worldwide's Head of Programmes, for her support.

Notes

1. Lionel Barber, editor of the *Financial Times*, and Jonathan Wheatley, Brazil correspondent, interviewed President Luiz Inácio Lula da Silva in London on 9 November 2009, www.ft.com/cms/s/0/e0357680-cbbf-11de-924d-00144feabdc0.html (accessed 8 November 2009).
2. Taken from the Editorial of *El Comercio*, Saturday 13 December 2008.
3. See 'Estudio de rentabilidad de los cultivos en los calles de la costa', CEPES-MINAG-FAO 2001, cited in Maranon and Moreyra (2009).
4. 'Direccion de Agronegocios of Ministry of Agricultural', www.peru.com/... /2009/4/1/DetalleDocumento_543353.asp (accessed November 2009).
5. This is part of an interview with FEPROMU in 2009.
6. Data collected through a focus group held by FEPROMU in March 2009.
7. Ana was interviewed by Rosa Asencio, Project Coordinator of the Young People Project. Fepromu, ICA February 2009.
8. Testimony collected by FEPROMU in 2009.

Bibliography

Burton, G. (2009) "Rapporteur's Report" Latin America and the Caribbean in the global financial crisis', Symposium, held at the Institute for the Study of the Americas, University of London, 21–22 April 2009, www.americas. sas.ac.uk/events/docs/EconomicCrisisPapers/RapporteurReport.pdf (last accessed November 2009).

Centro Peruano de Estudios Sociales (2009) 'La agroindustria se sindicaliza', *La Revista Agraria*, No. 110.

Maranon, B. and Moreyra, J. (2009) *La Agroindustria de Exportación no tradicional Frente a la Crisis Mundial*, Aurora Vivar, Lima, Peru.

About the author

Reineira Arguello is Programme Manager for Latin America at WOMANKIND Worldwide.

CHAPTER 7

Cheap and disposable? The impact of the global economic crisis on the migration of Ethiopian women domestic workers to the Gulf

Bina Fernandez

This chapter first appeared in *Gender & Development* 18(2), pp. 249–262, July 2010.

This chapter investigates the impact of the global economic crisis on the migration of Ethiopian women domestic workers to the Gulf. It argues that migration as a strategy to cope with existing crises in Ethiopia will be severely constrained by post-downturn policy shifts, which have already produced a significant decline in numbers of recorded migrants and remittances. Evidence suggests the consequence will be an increase in the flows of unrecorded migrants. The conclusion discusses policy responses to mitigate some of the negative consequences of the global economic crisis on the migration of Ethiopian domestic workers.

Introduction

Official estimates suggest that Ethiopians working abroad (both permanent and temporary) number between 800,000 and 1 million (National Bank of Ethiopia, 2006). In 2008, the recorded inflow of remittances from migrants was worth over US$800 million (National Bank of Ethiopia, 2008). Unofficial estimates suggest that the figures of unrecorded migrants and informal remittances are at least equivalent, if not higher.

Migrant remittances are crucial to the Ethiopian economy. The recorded remittances in 2007, of US$359 million surpassed the foreign direct investment (FDI) of US$223 million (World Bank, 2009). If flows through unofficial channels are accounted for, the International Monetary Fund (IMF) estimates that remittances contribute between 10 and 20 per cent of Ethiopia's US$13 billion annual gross domestic product (GDP) (Yau and Assefa, 2007; cited in Campbell, 2009: 19). The devaluation of the currency in late 2008 was a government measure to address inflation and a declining balance of payments, and also ensure the continued flow of remittances by making it more attractive for migrants to send money.

This chapter presents a case study of the impact of the economic crisis on the migration of Ethiopian women domestic workers to countries in the Middle East. In Ethiopia, migration has become an important strategy to cope with the multiple crises of recurrent famines, conflicts with neighbouring states, political represssion, and high unemployment that many Ethiopians have experienced over the past few decades.

The money sent by migrants working abroad makes a significant contribution to the ability of migrants' families and dependents to survive economic crises. It also contributes to the overall resilience of the national economy. How will the global economic crisis that began in September 2008 affect this? This chapter considers the possible answers to this question. The first section describes how Ethiopian women domestic workers end up working in the Middle East, discussing the channels and routes of migration. The second section discusses their experience of work, focusing on the two primary destinations of Saudi Arabia and Kuwait; the primary factors that 'pull' women domestic workers to these destinations; and the working conditions women experience there. The third section looks at the likely short- and long-term consequences of the economic crisis for this means of making a living. The final part of the chapter looks at the various responses to the crisis which are possible to protect migrant domestic workers from the potential negative consequences of the downturn, and emphasizes the importance of monitoring policy changes in the wake of the crisis in both Ethiopia and destinations in the Middle East.

An analysis of the impact of the global recession on the stocks and flows of Ethiopian emigrants and their remittances would require disaggregation by migrant destination countries, types of workers (legal or irregular, short- or long-term, male or female, skilled or unskilled) and sector of work being examined.

The chapter draws on primary research in Addis Ababa in two phases (April and July–August 2009). The objective of the research was to examine a migration trajectory that has received relatively little attention, and was prompted by my own observation of this phenomenon during my visits to Ethiopia. The research design included 15 semi-structured interviews conducted with return migrant women. These interviewees had all migrated for work already, at least once, and were now heading out on their second or third employment contracts. I found women to interview by three methods. First, employing a snowballing technique, women were contacted through personal networks. Second, contact was established with women via private employment agencies. Third, links were made with women who attended the pre-departure orientation sessions organized by the Ministry of Labour and Social Affairs (MOLSA). Informal group discussions with some of these women led to in-depth interviews with those who were willing. Additionally, 15 key interviews were conducted with the owners or managers of employment agencies and with government and non-government representatives.

Ethiopian women's migration to the Middle East

The initial surge of Ethiopian women's migration as domestic workers began to Lebanon, as early as 1989 (Beydoun, 2006). In 2008–2009, Saudi Arabia and Kuwait emerged as the top destination countries, absorbing 61 per cent and 33 per cent respectively of recorded Ethiopian migrant domestic workers. Most women migrants are employed in the service sector (primarily as domestic workers), and are from Asia (the Philippines, Indonesia and Sri Lanka). A growing number of migrant domestic workers in the Gulf Co-operation Council (GCC) are from Ethiopia, Eritrea, Sudan and Egypt (Sabban, 2002: 10), reflecting a shift to cheaper sources of labour.

The demand for migrant domestic workers can be explained first by the 'social compact' (Baldwin-Edwards, 2005: 27) between the Gulf monarchies and their populations, whereby the latter acquiesced in regime legitimacy as long as revenues from oil sales were used to subsidize state welfare systems since the 1970s (Nonneman, 2008: 6). The Gulf countries sanctioned the import of migrant labour for the 'dirty work' that nationals did not want – construction work and service sector work. Migrant domestic workers can thus be seen as part of an 'unspoken "bargain" between the state and the emerging civil society, by which the state provides a leisured life in exchange for complete political control' (Sabban, 2002: 11). Foreign domestic workers are a status symbol of this life of luxury, and are ordered in a racialized hierarchy, with Filipina women at the top signalling the highest status and commanding the highest salaries, followed by Indonesian and Sri Lankan women, and African women at the bottom.

The second contributory factor to the growth of the demand for migrant domestic workers is the Khafala system of short-term, contract migrant labour recruitment that is unique to the GCC countries. The Khafala is the sponsor-employer of migrants, without whom they are unable to obtain a work visa. Workers' legal presence in the country is tied to the Khafala, who invariably confiscates their passports in order to control them better, and they are unable to change employer. This leaves domestic workers particularly vulnerable, as they are isolated within homes. Despite the reported abuses, and calls for its abolition, the Khafala system flourishes because it is a lucrative business opportunity for ordinary citizens who engage in the business of selling sponsorships (Baldwin-Edwards, 2005), even if they are not direct employers, as well as for the migrant workers who enter the country under the system.

Routes of migration

There are three channels of migration to the Middle East. The first is 'public' migration, a misleading official label that is in contrast to the typical understanding of 'public' migration as government organization of migrant labour contracts with destination countries. Public migration in Ethiopia occurs when individuals are officially registered as migrant workers with MOLSA, but secure work contracts abroad through their personal contacts. The second channel is through one of the 110 legally registered 'private employment agencies' (PEAs). The PEAs secure contracts for domestic workers with employers in the Middle East, either directly or indirectly through recruiting agencies in the destination countries. Many PEAs unofficially charge women between 2,000 and 8,000 Ethiopian Birr (US$200–800) for their services, even though the cost of a return ticket, visa and insurance are supposed to be borne by the employer, and women are only supposed to pay for their passports and medical examination.

Together, the public and PEA channels constitute recorded migration from Ethiopia, as these migrant workers are required to register their employment contracts with MOLSA (personal communication from MOLSA, 2009). Currently, over 30,000 women annually pass through these two channels, accounting for 96 per cent of recorded labour migrants (MOLSA, 2009). Unofficial estimates by MOLSA officials during interviews indicate that an equivalent 30,000 migrants (at least) pass through the third channel of migration, using the services of illegal brokers. These illegal brokers may be individual operators, or legally registered companies that illegally provide employment brokerage services to migrants.

Both the PEA owners and illegal brokers are predominantly Muslims. Many of them are also traders involved in the (legal and illegal) import and export of commodities, travel and tourism, and informal financial services (*hawala*). They have used their trading networks to facilitate contacts with labour recruiting agencies in the Middle East, and thus diversify into the trade in people. These trade networks are based on trust, and the 'social capital' of personal, kin, language- and religion-based relationships (Little, 2005).

The importance of having prior trading links in the region is illustrated by the Ethiopian woman owner of Sabrine PEA (one of the oldest and largest agencies), who capitalized on the trade contacts of her Yemeni husband in the Middle East. As her husband stated: 'I am in the business of exporting cattle from Ethiopia, while my wife exports women – and let me tell you, it is easier to export cattle [because there are fewer government regulations to comply with]' (interview, April 2009, Addis Ababa). The importance of Muslim social networks was evident when an illegal broker interviewed said that although he was Christian, he went by the name Mohammed, and adopted Muslim greetings and behaviour when dealing with his contacts (interview, April 2009, Addis Ababa).

The legal migration route requires all women to register with MOLSA and provide proof of an employment contract, a work permit for the destination country, a medical examination certificate, and insurance. It is also possible for women legally to exit Ethiopia on tourist visas, or on Haj and Umrah visas to Saudi Arabia. They overstay their visa period, and either find an employer who will regularize their status in the destination country, or live and work illegally under the continuous threat of deportation. The majority of other undocumented migrants exit the country overland, via Dire Dawa and Hargesa in the south-east of Ethiopia, across to Bossasso on the coast of Somalia, and then overseas to Yemen (Endeshaw et al., 2006). Saudi Arabia is the intended destination of most of these undocumented migrants. However, the illegal brokers operating along this route are brutally exploitative, stripping prospective migrants of all their money and often abandoning them in the desert before they even reach the coast of Somalia. Large numbers of prospective migrants do not make it across to Yemen, and are deported back to Ethiopia before boarding the boats at Bossaso (ibid.). Many women who do manage to reach Yemen are marooned there, neither able to return to Ethiopia because of the exit fine payable to the Yemeni government because of their illegal migrant status in the country, nor able to undertake the even more dangerous and expensive next stage of the journey overland to Saudi Arabia (de Regt, 2007).

Who are the migrants, and why do they go?

A statistical profile of documented women migrant domestic workers from Ethiopia in 2008–2009 (MOLSA, 2009) reveals that:

- 91 per cent of the women were single
- 83 per cent were in the 20–30 age group
- 63 per cent had some secondary education, 26 per cent were illiterate
- 71 per cent were Muslim
- 93 per cent earned US$100–150 per month.

The profile of the typical migrant that emerges from official migration data is of young, unmarried Muslim women with some secondary education. All the women I interviewed said that seeing how friends and neighbours had benefited economically from migration provided strong motivation for them initially to embark on the journey. In Ethiopia, most of the population is occupied with earning a living in the informal economy, and there are very low employment prospects within the public sector for young women with secondary education. This, allied to the greater social acceptability for young Muslim women of employment within the private sphere of the household, and the lack of lucrative income-generating activities in the informal sector in Ethiopia leads many young Muslim women with secondary education to see migration as domestic workers as the best available economic opportunity. The network of Muslim agencies and brokers engaged in the trade in migrant labour plays a key role in facilitating the migration of these young women.

However, while the interviews and group discussions confirmed that most migrants were indeed young, unmarried Muslim women, I found that the total picture was more complex and nuanced. Orthodox Christian women were also seeking work as domestic workers. Some of them pretended to be Muslim while in employment, and one woman stated she was forcibly converted to Islam by her employer. I also interviewed two married Muslim women, who said they were going to Saudi Arabia to join their husbands, who were already working there.

A majority of the interviewees stated that they sent all, or nearly all, of their salary home, to support their ageing parents, siblings, and other family members. Their migration can thus be viewed as a family livelihood diversification strategy to cope with crisis. There is a strong cultural expectation that these young women should shoulder this responsibility. Some of the young women I interviewed had decided that since the first round of remittances had gone to their families, they would in future aim to keep some savings for themselves, to invest in a business on their return. Only three of the women had already made investments from their earnings – two had built houses that were rented out, while the third had opened a small shop. A couple of the interviewees, who appeared to be from better-off families, were free to spend their salaries as they wished, on clothes and gifts. The degree to which earning money as migrants was empowering for these women was, of course, mediated by their individual experiences of working conditions in the destination countries.

Destination Middle East: working conditions for domestic workers

Notwithstanding the stipulations of the work contract that ostensibly protect their rights as workers, the working conditions of Ethiopian women are similar to those of other migrant domestic workers in the Middle East (Human Rights Watch, 2008; Essim and Smith, 2004; Jureidini, 2003; Abou-Habib, 1998) and can be considered a form of 'contract slavery' (Bales, 2004; Jureidini and Moukarbel, 2004).

As live-in domestic workers, women reported, in the interviews I conducted in Addis Ababa, being on-call 24 hours a day, 7 days a week, and working between 10 and 20 hours daily. Some interviewees reported doing double duty – that is, cleaning or doing laundry for a second household, usually a relative of their employer. While some are fortunate to get half a day or a day off a week, many women get only one day off a month, or no break at all. Recounting her experience, one woman spoke of how her complete physical exhaustion from the lack of any break after four years working for a household in Dubai led to a mental breakdown, in which she was totally disoriented and could not tell what day of the week it was, or what time it was (interview, July 2009, Addis Ababa).

Verbal abuse by employers is commonplace, and several interviewees experienced racial insults and discriminatory behaviour (such as separate food and dishes for them) (interviews, April and July 2009, Addis Ababa). While physical abuse was not reported by any of the interviewees, they all asserted that other Ethiopians they knew had experienced physical and sexual abuse. Similarly, although none of the interviewees in this study reported wage exploitation, other studies document the non-payment or under-payment of wages to migrant domestic workers (Essim and Smith, 2004; Kebede, 2001).

Escaping from exploitative and abusive working conditions, some Ethiopian women become 'runaways'. They find shelter with other women, who live together in small rented rooms, and take on jobs as 'freelancers' – working as live-out domestic workers, brewing and selling illicit liquor, or engaging in sex work. Their lack of legal status makes them vulnerable to greater exploitation if they are detected, as they risk blackmail, imprisonment, and/or deportation. If they wish to leave voluntarily, they often have to pay high fines for exit visas. Notwithstanding these risks, they can often earn more, and have greater freedom of movement. However, the term 'runaway' was used in a pejorative sense by one Ethiopian government official and several of the PEA representatives during interviews, to describe these women as delinquents who abandon their contractual responsibilities because they do not want to work hard, and want an easy life.

In a significant policy move after several years of deliberation, in July 2009 the Shura Council of Saudi Arabia passed a bill that 'would require employers to give domestic workers at least nine hours of rest every day, suitable accommodation, and rest breaks' (Human Rights Watch, 2009). While this is a welcome initiative to protect the labour rights of migrant domestic workers, there are still concerns about ambiguous provisions of the bill such as the 'duty to obey employers' orders' and a prohibition against leaving the place of employment without a 'legitimate reason' (ibid.). In Kuwait too, after years of revisions, a proposed law introduced in December 2009 would be the first major update of Kuwait's 1964 Private Sector Labor Law. It heralds the abolishment of the Khafala sponsorship system and the establishment of a new agency to manage recruitment of migrant workers; although unfortunately, the legislation does not recognize domestic workers (Human Rights Watch, 2009). Future developments of these legislative initiatives in Saudi Arabia and Kuwait need to be closely monitored and analysed for their potential impact on Ethiopian migrant domestic workers.

The impact of the global downturn

Initially, the impact of the global downturn on the GCC countries was uncertain and mixed (Martin, 2009; Fix et al., 2009). However, the collapse of oil prices, and the contraction of international credit markets and global demand has led to a revision of the IMF growth projection for GCC countries, from 3.5 per cent in February 2009, to 1.3 per cent, with an expected shrinkage of the Saudi and Kuwait economies by 0.9 and 1.1 per cent respectively (Billing, 2009).

The global crisis has exacerbated an existing situation of high youth unemployment in the GCC countries, and a growing demand for nationalization of the workforce through the reduction of migration (Pakkiasamy, 2004). This has led to tightened control over the entry of migrant workers, particularly in Saudi Arabia, which has produced a drop in the numbers of Ethiopian women migrants since June 2009 (see Figure 7.1). In Saudi Arabia, the move towards 'Saudization' of the work force has led to the recruitment of Saudi women for the first time, as domestic workers (BBC News, 2009). However, though pressures for nationalization of the workforce might result in the tightening of borders to migrant workers in the short term, it is likely that over the long term, the demand for migrant domestic workers in the service sector would remain 'recession-proof'. Unlike the situation in the global North, this continued

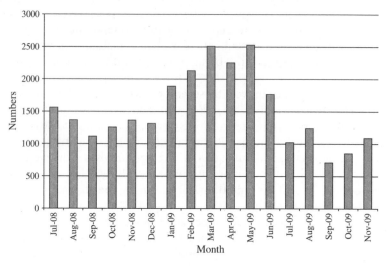

Figure 7.1 Documented Ethiopian migrant workers
Source: Ministry of Labour and Social Affairs

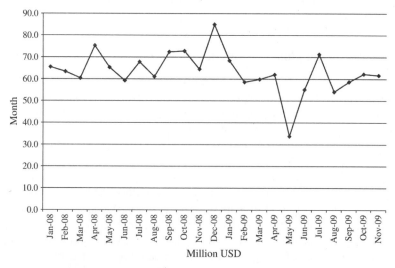

Figure 7.2 Private remittance transfers 2008–2009
Source: National Bank of Ethiopia

demand will currently be driven by the 'social compact' in GCC countries, rather than demographic changes, in particular because domestic work is considered shameful by citizens (ibid.), and there is a continuously expanding frontier of cheap labour from developing countries.

As argued earlier, migrant remittances are crucial to the Ethiopian economy. With the onset of the global recession, there has been a 20 per cent decline in recorded remittances from US\$812 million in 2008, to US\$645 million in 2009 according to data held by the National Bank of Ethiopia (see Figure 7.2).

The recorded remittances in 2007, of US\$359 million, surpassed the FDI of US\$223 million (World Bank, 2009). If flows through unofficial channels are accounted for, the IMF estimates that remittances contribute between 10 and 20 per cent of Ethiopia's US\$13 billion annual GDP (Yau and Assefa, 2007; cited in Campbell, 2009: 19). The devaluation of the currency in late 2008 was a government measure to address inflation and a declining balance of payments, and also ensure the continued flow of remittances by making it more attractive for migrants to send money.

A decline in remittances is not only a concern for Ethiopia's national accounts. At the household level, remittances in Ethiopia are used as a 'risk-sharing mechanism for self-insurance against shocks of various kinds' (Aredo, 2005; cited in Reinert, 2007: 78). Remittances are assuming greater significance during the global recession, as they provide a buffer for family survival at a time when soaring inflation has once again assailed the Ethiopian economy, particularly affecting food and fuel prices in the past year. This may partially account for the rise in the numbers of migrant workers in the initial months after the downturn (see Figure 7.1), as increasing numbers of women may have turned to migration as an alternative.

Now, more than ever, the regulation of migration and remittances – particularly unrecorded remittances – is firmly on the agenda of the Ethiopian government. In July 2009, the government introduced major amendments to the Private Employment Agency Proclamation of 1998, stating that its objective was to improve protection for migrant workers, in particular women.

However, the Ethiopian government lacks negotiating power with the governments of destination countries, and also lacks the ability to control illegal brokers. Hence, the measures for improved protection largely relate to increased regulation of the PEAs. In an interview, the manager of the Ethiopian Association of PEAs described the revised legislation as 'over-regulation', as it not only makes PEA owners pay a larger security deposit of between US\$30,000 and US\$50,000[1] in cash, but also makes them legally liable as employers for the women they recruit. He predicted that as a result of this squeeze on legal PEAs, it is likely that more of the trade in migrants will be driven underground: 'Almost three-fourths of the existing agencies cannot deposit this sum of money, so they would go underground and become illegal, rather than work as a legal agent' (interview, July 2009). Indications of the rise in the illegal border crossings are the recent UNHCR figures, documenting a 50 per cent increase in the numbers of people crossing the Gulf of Aden to Yemen. Over 74,000 people risked their lives to enter Yemen en route to Saudi Arabia in 2009, of which 42,000 were Ethiopians (*Fortune*, 2009).

A crackdown on illegal money exchangers is another recently introduced measure to 'capture' *hawala* transfers.

As a result of these dynamics, there is likely to be a future increase in the numbers of unrecorded migrants. First, rising prices in Ethiopia post-global downturn will make it likely that more women will seek migrant jobs, as this is a coping strategy undertaken by families to manage conditions of multiple internal crises (rising prices, unemployment, famine, political instability). Second, however, the recent legislative squeeze on legal PEAs and the post-downturn slowdown of legal migration to Saudi Arabia will produce a constriction in the legal channels of migration. This will produce a rise in the numbers of attempted migration through illegal routes, as there has been no significant amelioration of the conditions that generate the outflows of people.

Conclusion

The consequences may be that international migration can no longer be relied on as a buffer strategy to cope with existing crises of different kinds. The combined impact of rising prices and a substantial decline in remittances will mean that family survival will be under considerable pressure. Clearly, women in households will increasingly become the last resort buffers under these conditions. More women might seek employment in the informal sector, which may have a 'crowding out' effect of driving down the already low wages and remuneration in this sector. Within households, there may be deterioration in the nutritional and health status of women and girls, and a de-prioritisation of girls' education.

However, on the positive side, despite the fall in the numbers of migrant domestic workers to Saudi Arabia indicating that Ethiopian domestic workers might be more 'disposable' during the downturn, the 'social compact' in the Gulf countries suggests that this might be a short-term reversal. The demand for domestic workers, particularly Ethiopian ones, is likely to continue in the long-term, as they are 'cheaper' and perceived as more compliant than domestic workers from the Philippines and Indonesia.

Policy responses to mitigate some of the negative consequences of the global economic crisis on the migration of domestic workers need to be considered in both Ethiopia and the destination countries. Ethiopia first needs to focus on enhancing social protection measures such as direct assistance (through cash and asset transfers, school fee waivers) and insurance (health and unemployment) that would enhance the buffer capacity of families to withstand crises. While such measures might be limited owing to resource constraints of the Ethiopian government, low investment, small-win proposals could build on existing initiatives. Currently, MOLSA has a compulsory, pre-departure orientation programme for all registered migrant workers, and awareness-raising campaigns by the police and the Ministry of Women's Affairs inform prospective migrant domestic workers of the dangers of seeking employment abroad through illegal agents. Both programmes could be expanded and the co-ordination between these different government departments strengthened. Other proposals include support for an Ethiopian migrant women workers organization that would have branches in the destination countries, encouraging banks to make it easy for migrant women to open savings accounts and to transfer money to them, and strengthening the co-ordination between MOLSA and embassies in destination countries.

In the longer term, the Ethiopian government needs to consider whether to step up its role as a 'labour brokerage state' (Rodriguez, 2008), along the lines of the Philippines' Overseas Employment Administration Agency (POEA). In order to secure the interests of 1.5 million Filipino workers in over 190 countries, President Arroyo directed the POEA to adopt a strong proactive role and 'execute a paradigm shift by refocusing its functions from regulation to full-blast market development efforts' (POEA Annual Report; cited in Fix et al., 2009: 43–4). The establishment of an equivalent agency in Ethiopia, to invest in skills training of Ethiopian women and promote their employment in different countries, would strengthen the bargaining position of these women abroad.

Improving the employment conditions of Ethiopian migrant domestic workers in the Middle East assumes greater significance during an economic downturn, as the downturn may deepen the disregard for migrant women's rights as workers and human beings. The results may be a deterioration in working conditions, and an intensification of exploitative practices, such as being forced to work for two households for the same pay, or being denied wages. More women may also over-stay their visas and work permits in these countries, for fear of not being able to return legally, swelling the ranks of 'runaways' or undocumented workers. These women will be particularly at risk of deportation and abuse, particularly if there is a post-downturn intensification of xenophobia against foreign workers.

In GCC countries, the content of policies that would improve the working conditions of Ethiopian migrant domestic workers are the recognition and protection of the rights of domestic workers under labour and human rights law, reform of the Khafala system to allow for untied labour contracts, the decriminalization of 'runaways' and improved co-ordination with sending countries. These reforms are the minimal demands of advocates of policy change in the Gulf (Essim and Smith, 2004; Human Rights Watch, 2008), which must be vigorously re-emphasized at this juncture to prevent back-sliding during the downturn.

Whether the downward shift in flows of migration and remittances along this particular trajectory is short-term and cyclical, or long-term and structural, will depend largely on the combination of policies put in place in both sending and receiving countries. In either case, it is essential to monitor the policies introduced, and do a gender analysis of their potential consequences, to ensure migrant women workers do not disproportionately bear the negative consequences of the downturn.

Note

1. The bond is a financial guarantee that the PEA is expected to provide to the government, as an insurance against any costs of repatriation of workers that the government might have to bear. In the old legislation, it was possible to furnish this bond or guarantee from the financial institutions or insurance companies by mortgaging property (house or vehicle). According to the new draft, PEAs have to deposit the cash in the bank.

Bibliography

Abou-Habib, L. (1998) 'The use and abuse of female domestic workers from Sri Lanka in Lebanon', *Gender & Development* 6:1, pp. 52–56.

Baldwin-Edwards, M. (2005) *Migration in the Middle East and Mediterranean*, Global Commission on International Migration, Geneva, Switzerland.

Bales, K. (2004) *Disposable People: New Slavery in the Global Economy*, University of California Press, Berkeley, CA.

BBC News (2009) 'First Saudi women work as maids', www.bbcnews.co.uk (last accessed December 2009).

Beydoun, K.A. (2006) 'The trafficking of Ethiopian domestic workers into Lebanon: navigating through a novel passage of the international maid trade', *Berkeley Journal of International Law*, 24, pp. 1009–1045.

Billing, S. (2009) 'Saudi, Kuwait, UAE face 2009 recession – IMF', *Middle-East Business News*, www.arabianbusiness.com/555139-saudi-kuwait-uae-face-2009-recession-imf (last accessed December 2009).

Campbell, J.R. (2009) 'Caught between the ideology and realities of development, transiting from the Horn of Africa to Europe', Working Paper no. 2009/01, London School of Economics Migration Studies Unit, London.

de Regt, M. (2007) 'Ethiopian women in the Middle East: the case of migrant domestic workers in Yemen', paper presented at the African Studies Centre Seminar of 15 February, University of Amsterdam, www.ascleiden.nl/Pdf/paper-deregt.pdf (last accessed December 2009).

Endeshaw, Y., Gebeyehu, M. and Reta, B. (2006) *Assessment of Trafficking in Women and Children in and from Ethiopia*, International Organization for Migration, Addis Ababa.

Essim, S. and Smith, M. (eds) (2004) *Gender and Migration in Arab States, the Case of Domestic Workers*, International Labour Organisation, Regional Office for Arab States, Beirut.

Fix, M., Papademetriou, D., Batalova, J., Terrazas, A., Lin, S. and Mittelstadt, M. (2009) *Migration and the Global Recession*, Migration Policy Institute, Washington, DC, www.migrationpolicy.org (last accessed December 2009).

Fortune (2009) 'Ethiopians dominate flood of Africans to Yemen', *Fortune* 10:504, p. 24.

Human Rights Watch (2008) *As If I Am Not Human: Abuses against Asian Domestic Workers in Saudi Arabia*, www.hrw.org/en/reports/2008/07/07/if-i-am-not-human-0 (last accessed December 2009).

Human Rights Watch (2009) *Saudi Arabia: Shura Council Passes Domestic Worker Protections*, http://www.hrw.org/en/news/2009/07/10/saudi-arabia-shura-council-passes-domestic-worker-protections (last accessed December 2009).

Jureidini, R. (2003) 'Migrant workers and xenophobia in the Middle East', Identities, Conflict and Cohesion Programme Paper Number 2, United Nations Research Institute for Social Development, December.

Jureidini, R. and Moukarbel, N. (2004) 'Female Sri Lankan domestic workers in Lebanon: a case of "contract slavery"'?, *Journal of Ethnic and Migration Studies* 30:4, pp. 581–607.

Kebede, E. (2001) 'Ethiopia – an assessment of the international labour migration situation: the case of female labour migrants', GENPROM Working Paper No. 3, International Labour Organisation Geneva, Switzerland, www.ilo.org/employment/Whatwedo/Publications/lang--en/docName--WCMS_117931/index.htm, (last accessed December 2009).

Jureidini, R. (2003) 'Migrant workers and xenophobia in the Middle East', *Identities, Conflict and Cohesion Programme Paper Number 2*, United Nations Research Institute for Social Development (UNRISD), December 2003.

Little, P. (2005) 'Unofficial trade when states are weak: the case of cross-border commerce in the Horn of Africa', World Institute for Development Economics Research Working Paper no. 2005(13).

Martin, P. (2009) 'The recession and migration, alternative scenarios', Working Paper no. 13, International Migration Institute, James Martin 21st Century School, University of Oxford, UK.

National Bank of Ethiopia (2006) *Remittance Transfer Channels in Ethiopia*, National Bank of Ethiopia, Addis Ababa.

National Bank of Ethiopia (2008) *Annual Report*, National Bank of Ethiopia, Addis Ababa.

Nonneman, G. Ehteshami, A. and Wright, S.M. (eds) (2008) 'Political reform in the gulf monarchies, from liberalization to democratization? A comparative perspective', *Reform in the Middle East Oil Monarchies*, Ithaca Press, Reading, UK.

Pakkiasamy, S. (2004) *Saudi Arabia's Plan for Changing Its Workforce, Migration Information Source*, www.migrationinformation.org/USfocus/display.cfm?ID=264 (last accessed December 2009).

Reinert, K. (2007) 'Ethiopia in the world economy, trade, private capital flows, and migration', *Africa Today* 53:3, pp. 65–89.

Rodriguez, R.M. (2009) 'The labor brokerage state and the globalization of Filipina care workers', *Signs: Journal of Women in Culture and Society 2008*, 33:4, pp. 794–800.

Sabban, R. (2002) 'Migrant women in the United Arab Emirates: the case of female domestic workers', GENPROM Working Paper Series on Women and Migration no. 10, International Labour Organisation, Geneva, Switzerland, www.ilo.org/employment/Whatwedo/Publications/lang--en/doc Name--WCMS_117955/index.htm (last accessed December 2009).

World Bank (2009) World Bank Development Indicators, http://web.worldbank. org/WBSITE/EXTERNAL/DATASTATISTICS/0,,contentMDK:20519297~pa gePK:64133150~piPK:64133175~theSitePK:239419,00.html (last accessed December 2009).

About the author

Bina Fernandez is a lecturer in Development Studies at the University of Leeds.

CHAPTER 8

The effects of the global economic crisis on women in the informal economy: research findings from WIEGO and the Inclusive Cities partners

Zoe Elena Horn

This chapter first appeared in *Gender & Development* 18(2), pp. 263–276, July 2010.

Findings from a recent study on the impact of the economic crisis on informal workers in Asia, Latin America and sub-Saharan Africa reveal that transmission of the crisis to the informal economy is hitting poor women hard. Women constitute the majority of the informal workforce in most developing countries, and predominate its poorest and most vulnerable ranks. Evidence from four informal sectors suggests that income and employment trends during the crisis – decreasing demand and wages aggravated by rising competition – are strongest in the poorest-paying and lowest barrier-to-entry informal sectors and sub-sectors where women are concentrated. The crisis is compounding women's paid and unpaid informal work burden. As a result, the relative socio-economic vulnerability of poor working women and their families is deteriorating during the crisis.

Introduction

More than a year has passed since Wall Street's astonishing collapse, and international attention is now taken up by emerging signs of recovery in the world's wealthiest nations. Receiving relatively little attention, however, are new signs that the cost of the crisis is now being borne by those that can least afford it.

Like more than half of all women working today, Samuben Makwana, of Ahmedabad, India, is employed in the informal economy. The informal economy includes all economic units that are not recognized or regulated by the state, and all economically active persons who do not receive social protection through their work (International Labour Organization [ILO], 2002).[1] Samuben began working with mud at the age of 14. For the past 43 years, she has made her living mixing sand, water and cement, hauling brick and stone, and digging ditches, at construction sites across Ahmedabad, India. In good times, contractors paid Samuben US$3.10 a day for her labour. Today, the ailing economy in Ahmedabad has caused construction projects to grind to a halt, and there are virtually no new jobs in this sector. Samuben, the primary provider for her family, has no recourse in these desperate times.

There is a significant overlap between being a woman, working in the informal sector, and being poor (Chen, 2001). Over the past several decades, employment in the informal economy has risen rapidly across the developing world. The trend is for relations between employers and employees to become increasingly informal and casual, in terms of contracts and conditions of work. This trend has been closely linked to another: women are increasingly finding that they are the main or chief breadwinners in families where men cannot find work which conforms to social stereotypes of 'men's work'. The informal economy is the primary source of employment for women in most developing countries, and most women are concentrated in the most temporary, low-paying, and insecure jobs within it. Informally employed women frequently work under extremely precarious circumstances for very low wages, and without benefits or social protection.

The ILO estimates that employment in the informal economy comprises over half of all employment in Latin America, over 70 per cent in sub-Saharan Africa, and 65 per cent of non-agricultural employment in Asia. Other estimates have put the proportion closer to 80 per cent (ILO, 2002).

The already very high percentage of informally employed women is expected to rise during the current downturn. Evidence from past crises suggests the ranks of the informally employed swell during economic crises, because many retrenched workers and formal wage earners take up informal activities to compensate for the loss or decline of wages and purchasing power (Lee, 1998; Tokman, 1992). This income from informal work is particularly critical for poor working women, who, even at the best of times, have the most insecure employment and the slimmest margins for survival.

Yet, despite the size and significance of the informal economy, and the fact that it is particularly important to women workers, global media attention and policy responses have largely focused on the impact – in its various different forms – of the economic, financial and employment crises in male-dominated formal sectors. There has been little attention paid to the impact of the current downturn on the informal economy, or its female workforce.

Contrary to common assumptions, the informal economy does not serve as a safety net or 'cushion' for its formal counterpart during economic downturns; and informal workers, lacking social and economic protections, have no cushion of their own. While the number of informally employed women, as well as men, may rise during the crisis, this does not necessarily mean that either traditional, long-term informal workers, or new entrants, are thriving. Rather, as this article argues, the current global economic crisis is actually driving informally employed women and their families further into impoverishment. The article uses recent evidence from four informal occupational sectors – construction work, home-based work, street-vending and waste-picking – across Africa, Latin America and sub-Saharan Africa.

The article looks at the ways in which the crisis has been transmitted to poor women and their households in developing countries, and explores poor women's relative economic and social vulnerability during the crisis. It traces the different effects of the crisis on women living in poverty and their dependents, referring to these as first- and second-round effects. First-round effects are changes to women's share of informal occupations, in comparison to that of men, and changes to the status of this work. Second-round effects are the effects that first-round changes have on workers' households. Here, the loss of women's income during crisis plays out with long-term negative implications for the welfare of poor families, both because of women's contribution to household income and their 'preference' to invest scarce resources on child well-being and, therefore, on future development (Buvinic, 2009). Finally, in order to address the effects of the economic crisis on informally employed women, this article provides policy recommendations aimed at local, national, and international actors positioned to provide assistance to informal workers and their families.

The research

This chapter is based on findings from an ongoing global study[2] conducted by the Inclusive Cities project, and coordinated by Women in Informal Employment Globalizing and Organizing (WIEGO). The study aimed to fill the current gap in information about the impact of the crisis on informally employed workers in three regions – Asia and Latin America and sub-Saharan Africa.

Study research was conducted between July and September 2009, by local and regional member-based organizations of informal workers, as well as several technical support organizations that work directly with the working poor. Data were gathered through focus-group discussions, one-on-one interviews with workers, and key informant interviews. Key informant interviews were conducted with informal sector specialists as well as organizers and coordinators directly involved with informal workers' member-based organizations.

This chapter draws on data from 16 focus groups, whose participants were each interviewed individually. In total, 219 informal workers were interviewed from 4 occupational sectors: 12 construction workers, 102 home-based workers, 52 street vendors, and 53 waste-pickers. In all sectors, the majority of participants are women, who represented 82 per cent of the total number of research participants.

The findings

First-round effects: income and employment trends for women in four informal sectors

Over the past few decades, much of the process of informalization and feminization[3] of the labour forces in developing countries (Charmes, 2001) has been related to the growth of home-based work and export manufacturing.[4]

Recently, demand has decreased for home-based workers' products. Labour-intensive export products such as toys, textiles and garments, footwear and leather products, electronics and auto parts have been severely affected (Dejardin and Owens, 2009). Between September 2008 and February 2009, exports fell at an annualized rate of about 70 per cent in emerging Asia (that is, China, India, Hong Kong SAR, Korea, Singapore, Taiwan Province of China, Indonesia, Malaysia, the Philippines, Thailand, and Viet Nam) (International Monetary Fund [IMF], 2009). This has particularly affected many who have been working under sub-contracting arrangements. Sixty per cent of sub-contracted participants reported that they had received smaller and more infrequent contracts from middlemen[5] in the previous six months. Decreased production and fewer hours of work left 64 per cent of sub-contracted workers reporting diminished incomes (IMF, 2009).

Reduced demand for exports has also weakened the market for the recyclables used in the production and packaging of export goods, particularly those from China. This began to influence international pricing dynamics as early as October 2008. Waste-pickers are, consequently, highly vulnerable during economic crises, as losses are often transferred disproportionately to those – including waste-pickers – at the bottom of local and global supply chains. Indeed, the waste-pickers in this study reported the sharpest decline in demand and selling prices among the investigated sectors. Between January and June 2009, reported prices for waste materials had, on average, dropped between 5 and 7 per cent for those picking waste in Pune, India, while the prices dropped by as much as 42 per cent and 50 per cent in Bogotá, Colombia, and Santiago, Chile, respectively. Although waste-pickers in Pune, India, registered less-dramatic price drops, 77 per cent of them reported a decline in their income during the period of investigation. Participants reported that reduced consumption locally, owing to tough economic times, was leaving less waste for pickers to collect. The co-operative scrap shop where these workers sold their material registered an almost 50 per cent drop in the total volume of material they brought for sale.[6]

In many developing countries, a clear majority of waste-pickers on streets and dumps are women and children. Women waste-pickers scavenge for waste materials that have a resale value, while men are more likely to be involved in the processing and selling of this recovered material, and are more likely to be middlemen and managers (Furedy, 1990). Waste-pickers typically receive a very small percentage of the price that industry pays for the materials – those in Indian cities receive as little as 5 per cent (Medina, 2005). Women are often paid less than men for the waste materials they sell, and receive less by way of advances or loans from middlemen (Muller and Scheinberg, 2003).

As workers' wages fall in developing countries, retrenched and under-employed workers are curbing their consumption, even when it comes to cheaper goods. Of the street vendors participating in the study, 62 per cent reported that their volume of trade had dropped since January 2009.

A combination of fewer customers and higher business costs has taken a toll on street vendors. Of the participants in the study, 77 per cent reported that their weekly profit had decreased between January and June 2009.

Many traders also reported rising business costs, such as the price of raw materials, or the cost of ready-made goods, transportation, utilities, and market fees.[7] While 83 per cent of street vendors reported increased business costs since January 2009, only 58 per cent reported increasing the prices of their goods over the same period to offset their losses. Instead, many traders feared losing additional customers and, instead of raising prices, opted for reducing costs, by keeping less stock, lowering the quality of their goods, and/or limiting the variety of their products. Such strategies add risk and uncertainty to trade, and may heighten economic vulnerability over the long term. This state of affairs is particularly worrying for female street vendors, who are already more likely than men to operate in insecure or illegal spaces, to trade in less profitable goods, to generate a lower volume of trade, and to work as commission agents or employees of other vendors.

Declining income among customers in local markets is also having an impact on those who make their own products for sale at home, through family businesses or own-account operations. Eighty-four per cent of self-employed home-based workers reported that their monthly incomes had fallen during the first half of 2009. Unlike sub-contracted home-based workers, these workers have no middlemen to provide them with work orders. Instead, self-employed home-based workers, particularly those involved in food production, often sell their goods directly to their customers, through market stalls or from their home. Of the self-employed home-based workers participating in the study, 75 per cent reported that the volume of their trade had decreased in the preceding six months. However, lower demand or a decreased volume of sales did not translate into decreased work hours among the self-employed. Rather, one-third (34 per cent) were working longer hours to maintain their profit margins.

Women's employment is often more precarious than men's employment in both the formal and informal economy, and this leads to greater vulnerability and lower earnings in times of crisis. Compared with the male informal work-force, women are more likely to be own-account workers and sub-contracted workers, and are less likely to be owner-operators or paid employees of informal enterprises. When employment opportunities are scarce, women tend to be more willing than men to accept lower-paying, more irregular and more inse-cure work (Dejardin and Owens, 2009). Thus, women are often concentrated in informal sectors where barriers to entry are often low. During crises, these are the sectors which become swollen by newly retrenched and underemployed workers.

Most women involved in the study reported that new entrants in their sector were mostly other women. The vast majority – 85 per cent – of street vendors reported more competition, in already over-crowded vending areas, between January and July 2009. Over one-third of self-employed and sub-contracted home-based workers also reported increased numbers of workers in their sectors during the previous six months (34 per cent and 36 per cent respectively). Nearly half reported that the price they receive for their products (paid at 'piece rate' – that is, per unit) had fallen in the previous six months. In these conditions, piece-rates (the normal form of payment for these workers) can be driven very low, even though they are often highly skilled.

Women are also disproportionately concentrated in unskilled sub-sectors of work, which often decreases their competitiveness against new male entrants. This can potentially crowd out women, pushing them into more poorly paid jobs, or unpaid market work (Dejardin and Owens, 2009). Displaced male workers from the formal economy have start-up capital from severance pay and/ or savings; this poses a threat. Women are also particularly under threat from new male entrants in physically demanding occupations. These effects were evident among women construction workers from Ahmedabad, India, where the activist organization, the Self-Employed Women's Association (SEWA) estimates the decline of key industries such as diamond polishing during the crisis resulted in a 25 per cent surge in those seeking informal construction work (SEWA, 2009). Many of these new entrants, both men and women, are competing for work in unskilled construction work, as the barriers to entry are lower. This disproportionately affects women, who are already concentrated in unskilled construction work, such as hauling cement, or staining and sanding. Men, on the other hand, are more likely to be skilled in areas such as masonry, plumbing, and tile work.

New male entrants in construction not only possess physical advantages over their female counterparts, but they also have the advantage of being able to devote increased time and attention to their work, free from the many unpaid care and work obligations experienced by their female competitors in the labour market.

To examine the case of construction workers in Ahmedabad in more detail: with fewer household duties, men seeking construction work are generally able to arrive earlier at the recruitment corners (*kadiya naka*), where most construction workers gather each day to compete for construction jobs. New female construction workers are less likely to have the necessary training to compete for skilled construction jobs, and because of cultural norms, men are more likely to be selected for any on-site training. Unfortunately, neither new entrants nor traditional construction workers have promising prospects in Ahmedabad. The economic downturn and the high cost of building materials have curbed local construction, and construction workers reported that their monthly work days had fallen from 10–15 days to 5–6 days of work a month. Daily earnings, however, have fallen disproportionately for unskilled workers. In February 2009, unskilled workers received 100–150 rupees a day for their labour, but at the time of their interviews in August 2009 were receiving 70–80 rupees per day. Skilled workers received 200–250 rupees a day, in both February and August 2009. Consequently, the crisis is intensifying the movement of women into both unskilled and lower-paying work, forcing them further to the margins of their sector.

Second-round effects: increasing vulnerability of informally employed women and their households

The vulnerability of households to the effects of an economic crisis depends on the assets that they can call on. In order to achieve and maintain a solid asset base, it is essential to have a stable flow of income from a variety of sources. Research participants had an average of two income earners in their households, to support six family members. Nearly 40 per cent of female respondents were the primary income earner in their household, and in other households women's incomes were critical to sustaining their household income levels.

During the crisis, this income-earning burden for women may be intensifying. In families with multiple earners, the income from additional earners often came from the same parts of the informal economy as the respondent's income. Thus, the effects of the economic crisis on income and employment were compounded for these families. In addition, 20 per cent of respondents reported the recent retrenchment of a household member during the previous six months, and twice as many (40 per cent) reported a dramatic decrease in the income provided of one or more household members over the same period. Increasing numbers of informally employed women are now caring for entire families on less income.

During non-crisis times, women's earnings from paid work are a critical source of subsistence to themselves and their families, as spending on food, childcare and other household needs are often managed entirely by women. Yet, these women are also disadvantaged by social security schemes linked to their labour market status (Cichon and Hegemejer, 2007). Without access to these safety nets during the crisis, poor women substitute their own paid and unpaid informal work in order to maintain their families' living standards during a downturn (Moser, 1996). Despite the absence of opportunities, informal women reported increasing their work effort during the period of investigation out of concern for the well-being of their families, and their children in particular.

Coping strategies are often risky, and some have a long-term impact on human development, which reminds us of the role of women as gatekeepers in the inter-generational transfer of poverty (Knowles et al., 1999). Women commonly balanced budgets by cutting back on spending on personal and household needs. In poor families, food is typically allocated a large share of the household budget. During the crisis, respondents reported reducing both the quantity and quality of food served to their families; fewer meals are being served, while 'luxury' items such as milk and meat are being cut. Compounding income short-falls, staple food prices in many developing countries have remained higher even as world prices have fallen, and in many cases, are higher than a year ago when world prices were at their peak (WFP, 2009). While the origin of these price increases precedes the economic crisis, the ongoing impacts of the food and fuel crises are contributing to the pressure on household incomes.[8]

During crises, women struggle more to feed their families, while still having to maintain unpaid care and domestic chores (ILO, 2009a). Among female home-based workers, 27 per cent of respondents reported that they were the primary earner in their household, and the majority of these workers carried out childcare duties alongside their home-based production. Women participating in the study also carried out a disproportionate amount of domestic work in their households, such as preparing family meals, cleaning the house, washing clothes, and providing hospitality to guests. Sadly, decreased incomes have meant that some women cannot afford the few conveniences that would lighten their load. A woman in Thailand reported that she could no longer buy prepared meals for her family, which had saved her time and energy in the past. Consequently, her unpaid domestic work has further constrained this woman's options for paid work. Some respondents also reported cutting back on educational and medical expenses.

Three-quarters of respondents had children aged under 16 years in their households, with an average of two children in these households. While respondents reported having difficulty in paying for school fees and other educational expenses, few respondents reported removing their children from school altogether. Arguably, limited school drop-out rates reflect the fact that families are trying to protect what is perhaps the most important type of investment they can make – namely, their children. However, the length and severity of the economic crisis may push some families to the brink of desperation, and in this case, evidence from past crises show that female children are likely to be withdrawn from school first.

Although health services are generally considered a luxury at the best of times, many informal workers have physically demanding and health-compromising work environments. Some home-based workers in Pakistan, who regularly injure their hands during their work, reported foregoing prescription medicines for cheaper and less effective treatments. They expressed concern that these home remedies would affect their long-term earnings, because their fingers are the tools of their trade.

Despite their strategies to balance budgets, some workers resorted to borrowing from neighbourhood storekeepers, or local moneylenders. Some waste-pickers borrowed from scrap-shop owners, while home-based workers in Thailand reported borrowing from moneylenders to pay the debts piling up from other moneylenders. In these informal credit markets, workers were being charged upwards of 30 per cent a month in interest. These interest payments increase financial pressure on informal workers, and reduce their earnings over the long term. The enormous pressure being exerted on informal workers was taking a toll on respondents' emotional resources. Participants reported feeling depressed and exhausted. Much of the depression was linked to feelings of failure and disappointment in providing for their children. Workers were also sensitive to rising levels of insecurity and depression among their family members, which increased their sense of guilt.

Policy implications

Informal workers need assistance now. Global and national policymakers have invested tremendous resources into interventions that have helped stem the effects of the crisis on some of the world's most powerful economic actors, but top-down solutions will not be sufficient to help those struggling at the bottom of the global economic pyramid right now.

In addition, the worst may also still lie ahead for many informal workers. In the wake of the crisis, potential future cuts to national budgets and international aid will adversely affect the poor, and women will be particularly strained by cuts to public spending in areas related to family welfare (United Nations Development Fund for Women [UNIFEM], 2009). Women tend to be the least visible and most vulnerable in the informal economy, and, yet, are often the most powerful economic and social agents in their households and communities. Women can play a particularly important role as agents of change in this respect. For this reason, governments in developing countries must act now to prioritize expenditures in order to support pro-poor, gender-sensitive policies that will, at their core, promote the livelihoods of the majority of their workforce.

In their efforts to address the ongoing impact of the economic crisis, government authorities and international specialists must develop public policies through a participatory process that engages poor women and informal workers in the design and implementation of these measures. With their input, sector-specific bailouts should be developed to help informal workers maintain existing employment opportunities during the crisis, or secure new employment opportunities once it has ended. These policies would be more responsive to the specific needs in each sector, and will more effectively mitigate the effects of the crisis. This does not necessarily require additional spending, but reallocation of spending and adjustment of policies. In order to be effective, these crisis-response policies must also be informed by the short-, medium-, and long-term view. While responses will be context-specific, it is possible to make a number of broad recommendations with these issues in mind.

Emergency relief measures to break the crippling cycle of personal and household debt, aggravated by the crisis, should be a priority. Expanding economic opportunities for poor women should be a core theme of public works and other safety nets, including incentives and skills development for women. One example is the National Rural Employment Guarantee Act in India, passed in 2005, which guarantees employment to adult members of every rural household in India for at least 100 days in every financial year.[9] Similar schemes could be implemented on a short-term emergency basis, targeted at specific sectors of informal workers, and the working poor in hard-hit areas. Also, cash transfer programmes targeted at specific informal sectors should be accompanied by existing cash transfer programmes speeding up dispersal of their funds, without conditions being attached. Micro-finance institutions should also focus on offering credit and other financial services to poor borrowers, the majority of whom are women (Sabarwal et al., 2009).

In both the short and medium term, barriers to informal activities should be reduced under the principle of 'do no harm'. Laws, rules, and regulations undermining the livelihoods of informal workers, particularly women and working mothers, should be suspended, at least temporarily. Informal workers who have no income-earning alternatives must be permitted to make a living and support their families through the crisis. For home-based workers, this could involve suspension of policy biases that favour formal firms and workers over informal firms, and workers in access to government contracts for such items as school uniforms and hospital linens. For construction workers and informal waste-pickers, this could include cessation of harassment by authorities. Appropriate government agencies should also ensure that existing labour laws are applied fairly to women workers, and guard against exploitation during the crisis.

Social safety nets help mitigate the adverse effects of the crisis by relieving the burden of unpaid care work on women and girls. Even in non-crisis times, spending on social safety nets in developing countries is insufficient to meet needs (World Bank, 2009). Where public services exist, governments must ensure the continued financing of essential services like access to health and education. In the longer term, sustaining support for workers necessitates expanding and improving social protection programmes that better serve the needs of informal workers and their dependents. This could be achieved through specially designed social insurance schemes, as well as the extension and reform of formal sector social insurance.

The crisis also presents an opportunity for governments and other actors to re-think economic models and policies, and institute long-term, meaningful policy reform toward the informal economy. In particular, the mainstreaming – or 'formalization' – of the informal workforce should be reframed as a process aimed at increasing earnings and reducing risks for the working poor, not simply registration and taxation of informal enterprises. The working poor in the informal economy need to be *visible* in economic statistics and policies, have a *voice* in economic decision-making, and be seen as having *validity*, or legitimacy, as economic agents and targets of economic policies.

Conclusion

The idea of the informal economy as a safety net is an illusion. Global recession undermines the precarious livelihoods of the traditional informal workforce and the ability of new entrants to find shelter in the informal economy (Grant, 2006). Transmission of the downturn to informal sectors is hitting poor women particularly hard. Women constitute the majority of the informal workforce in most developing countries, and predominate its poorest and most vulnerable ranks. Trends of decreasing demand and wages, aggravated by rising competition, are strongest in the poorest-paying parts of the informal economy, which have the lowest barriers to entry, and where women are concentrated.

Informal workers have no cushion of economic and social protection to fall back on. Instead, poor workers – and in particular women – are substituting their own paid and unpaid labour, to maintain their families' living standards. As a result, women's economic, physical and emotional burdens are being compounded during the crisis, and the relative socio-economic vulnerability of poor working women and their families is worsening. This reality is particularly grim given that, in the formal sector, recovery from unemployment is expected to lag that of growth, and the ILO's bleakest employment predictions may yet become reality: an estimated worldwide rise of 51 million people between 2007 and the end of 2009 (ILO, 2009b), with 22 million of these newly-unemployed workers being women (ILO, 2009c).

On the long road to sustainable economic recovery from this crisis, supporting the livelihoods of poor working women and mobilising their leadership will ultimately be critical to improving the lives of the poorest, most vulnerable and hardest-hit women, men and children in the developing world.

Notes

1. In this chapter, employment in the informal economy includes all paid work inside and outside informal enterprises – both self-employment and wage employment – that is not recognized, regulated, or protected by existing legal or regulatory frameworks, as well as unpaid work in income-producing enterprises.

2. The Inclusive Cities project was launched in late 2008, with the aim of improving the livelihoods of the urban working poor, most of whom are employed in the informal economy. Inclusive Cities addresses urban poverty through providing support to, and building capacity of, membership-based organizations (MBOs) of the working poor in the urban informal economy. Inclusive Cities aims to strengthen MBOs in the areas of organizing, policy analysis, and advocacy, in order to ensure that urban informal workers have the tools necessary to make themselves heard within urban planning processes. Inclusive Cities is a global collaborative project with the following partners: Asiye eTafuleni, AVINA, Homenet South Asia, Homenet South-East Asia, KKPKP, the Latin America Network of Wastepickers (Recicladores Sin Fronteras), SEWA, StreetNet International and WIEGO. More information is available on the project website at www.inclusivecities.org.

3. The 'feminization' of the labour market refers to shifting patterns of women's labour participation – associated with globalization – that mark not only a rise of women's participation in the labour market, but also an increased segmentation of the labour market by gender. Women are increasingly participating in paid work but these women are, in turn, increasingly concentrated in precarious and low-paying sectors and sub-sectors of the economy.
4. For a review of this evidence, also see Chen et al. (1999).
5. The term 'middlemen' can be applied to individuals or firms, often them-selves informal, who operate further up the value chain from informal workers or enterprises and who act as points of access (and barrier) for entry of their goods to international, regional or local markets.
6. Pune waste-pickers who collect waste from Infosys sell their material to a cooperative scrap store run by their own organization, KKPKP. Those who service Pune University Campus are under a formal contract between KKPKP and the University, and earn a salary, apart from the money they receive through sale of scrap. Scrap is usually accumulated for a week and then sold collectively by the group and the profits are shared equally after deducting expenses.
7. While fee hikes by authorities and private market operators may not have the deliberate intention of intensifying the crisis, these actions are none-theless making business more expensive for vendors when they can least afford it.
8. According to the World Food Program, in 78 percent of the countries covered by their price monitoring bulletin, the cost of a basic food basket during April–June 2009 was higher than the same period in 2008 (UN Food and Agriculture Organization [FAO], 2009).
9. For more information on the NREGA, please see MacAuslan (2008).

References

Buvinic, M. (2009) 'The global financial crisis: assessing vulnerability for women and children, identifying policy responses', paper presented at the 53rd Session of the UN Commission on the Status of Women New York.

Charmes, J. (2001) 'Informal sector, poverty and gender: a review of empirical evidence', background paper for *World Development Report 2001*, World Bank Washington, DC.

Chen, M. (2001) 'Women in the informal sector: a global picture, the global movement', *SAIS Review*, 21:1, pp. 71–82.

Chen, M., Sebstad, J. and O'Connell, L. (1999) 'Counting the invisible work-force: the case of homebased workers', *World Development*, 27:3, pp. 603–610.

Cichon, M. and Hegemejer, K. (2007) 'Changing the development paradigm: investing in a social security floor for all', *International Social Security Review* 60: 2–3, pp. 169–196.

Dejardin, A.K. and Owens, J. (2009) 'Asia in the global economic crisis: impacts and responses from a gender perspective', paper presented at the ILO High-level Regional Forum on Responding to the Economic Crisis – Coherent Policies for Growth, Employment and Decent Work in Asia and the Pacific Manila, Philippines.

Furedy, C. (1990) 'Social aspects of solid waste recovery in Asian cities', *Environmental Sanitation Review* 30, pp. 2–52.

Grant, U. (2006) 'Urban economic growth and chronic poverty', background paper for the Chronic Poverty Report 2008–09, Chronic Poverty Research Centre, Manchester, UK.

ILO (2002) *Women and Men in the Informal Economy: A Statistical Picture*, ILO, Geneva, Switzerland.

ILO (2009a) 'Gender equality at the heart of decent work: interview with Jane Hodges', *World of Work*, (ILO Magazine) 65, www.ilo.org/wow/Articles/lang-en/WCMS_105183/index.htm (last accessed 4 June 2010).

ILO (2009b) *Global Employment Trends: January 2009*, ILO, Geneva, Switzerland.

ILO (2009c) *Global Employment Trends for Women: March 2009*, ILO, Geneva, Switzerland.

IMF (2009) *Regional Economic Outlook: Asia and Pacific*, IMF, Washington, DC.

Knowles, J., Pernia, E. and Racelis, M. (1999) 'Social consequences of the financial crisis in Asia', Asian Development Bank Economic Staff Paper no. 60, Manila, ADB Philippines.

Lee, E. (1998) *The Asian Financial Crisis: The Challenge for Social Policy*, ILO, Geneva, Switzerland.

MacAuslan, I. (2008) 'India's National Rural Employment Guarantee Act: A case study for Oxfam International', Oxford, UK.

Medina, M. (2005) 'Waste picker cooperatives in developing countries', paper presented at the WIEGO/Cornell/SEWA Conference on Membership-Based Organizations of the Poor, Ahmedabad, India, 17–21 January 2005.

Moser, C. (1996) *Confronting Crisis: A Comparative Study of Household Responses to Poverty and Vulnerability in Four Poor Urban Communities*, Environmentally Sustainable Development Studies and Monographs Series no. 8, Washington, DC: World Bank.

Muller, M. and Scheinberg, A. (2003) 'Gender-linked livelihoods from modernising the waste management and recycling sector: a framework for analysis and decision making', in V. Maclaren and N. Thi Anh Thu (eds) *Gender and the Waste Economy: Vietnamese and International Experiences*, National Political Publisher, Hanoi, Viet Nam.

Sabarwal, S., Sinha, N. and Buvinic, M. (2009) 'The global financial crisis: assessing vulnerability for women and children', World Bank Policy Brief, World Bank, Washington, DC.

SEWA (2009) *Financial Crises & Employment Melt Down in Informal Economy: SEWA's Experience and Implications*, SEWA, Ahmedabad, India.

Tokman, V.E. (1992) *The Informal Sector in Latin America*, Lynne Rienner Publishers, Boulder, CO.

UN FAO (2009) *Crop Prospects and Food Situation April 2009*, FAO, Rome, Italy.

UNIFEM (2009) 'Making economic stimulus packages work for women and gender equality', UNIFEM Working Paper, June.

World Bank (2009) 'Protecting progress: the challenge facing low-income countries in the global recession', background paper presented at the G-20 Leaders' Meeting Pittsburgh, PA.

World Food Programme (WFP) (2009) *The State of Food Insecurity in the World 2009*, WFP, Rome.

About the author

Zoe Elena Horn is a project coordinator and researcher for WIEGO. She is currently coordinating WIEGO's ongoing global study on the impact of the economic crisis on the informal economy.

CHAPTER 9

How the global economic crisis reaches marginalized workers: the case of street traders in Johannesburg, South Africa

Jennifer Cohen

This chapter first appeared in *Gender & Development* 18(2), pp. 277–289, July 2010.

This chapter explores the effects of liberal macroeconomic policies and the economic crisis on informal street traders. Street traders are linked to financial markets and the crisis primarily though demand conditions: slower growth and over-trading translate into lower profits. Field research indicates that female traders' households rely significantly more than male traders' households on income generated by trading.

Introduction

Traders in the informal economy are often perceived by policymakers as existing on the margins of national economies, and thus not affected, or minimally affected, by macroeconomic policy decisions. However, research suggests that demand for traders' products fluctuates depending upon macroeconomic dynamics, and that traders' livelihoods are directly linked to global value chains, albeit typically at the least profitable end (Velia et al., 2006; Webster et al., 2008). Studies also indicate that 'coping strategies' which are, in reality, unsustainable desperation measures, for dealing with a changing trading environment are very limited, rendering traders among the most vulnerable workers.

This chapter examines the case of informal street traders in Johannesburg, South Africa, who sell new clothing. Some economists and policymakers have claimed that the South African informal economy is structurally disconnected from the formal economy and is largely unaffected by formal economy phenomena (Mbeki, 2003; Reynolds and van Zyl, 2006). In fact, the research on which this article draws shows that South African street traders are directly affected by the country's macroeconomic policies of liberalization, and the economic crisis which began in the USA.

Informal activity constitutes one-half to three-quarters of non-agricultural work in underdeveloped countries (Chen, 2007). Hart (1976) coined the term 'informal economy' to describe his observations of urban employment in Ghana. The informal economy refers to a diverse set of economic activities, ranging from insecure, sub-contracted piecework done at home and domestic labour to more entrepreneurial-type self-employment (Peterson, 2003). Skinner (2005) notes that although different criteria are emphasized by different authors, the common understanding that they share of informal economic activity is that it tends to be relatively small scale and 'elude[s] certain government requirements such as registration, tax and social security obligations and health and safety regulations for workers'.

South Africa has a relatively small informal economy, given the scale of unemployment identified by the South African labour force surveys (LFS). According to the 16th LFS,[1] conducted in September 2007, South Africa's official unemployment rate is 23 per cent.[2] An expanded definition of unemployment that includes discouraged work-seekers raises the unemployment statistic to 35.8 per cent.[3] The survey estimates formal employment at 42.6 per cent of the labour force and informal employment at 10.3 per cent of the labour force. According to most studies, the majority of workers in the informal economy are men, but women predominate in certain sectors, like street trading in fruits and vegetables (Skinner, 2005; World Bank, 2002). Between 50 and 70 per cent of informal employment in South Africa is in wholesale or retail trade (Statistics South Africa, 2007). Retail trading includes businesses selling food, clothing, cigarettes, compact discs, mobile phone accessories, and so on.

The global economic crisis and Bree Street traders

According to orthodox economists, South Africa's macroeconomic policies have been good; its 'sophisticated financial system is fundamentally sound' as of August 2008, according to the International Monetary Fund (IMF) (2008: 3). These economists have historically advocated financial liberalization, reasoning that supposedly efficient capital markets provide discipline, 'rewarding good policies and penalizing bad' (Fisher, 1998: 3). South Africa adopted 'good', orthodox, policies in the 1990s, and liberalized its capital account, but its reward for these efforts has been integration into the 'New Financial Architecture' and the detrimental impacts of the global economic crisis (Crotty, 2009).

While countries with banks not holding toxic debt may have escaped the immediate fallout, they are subject to significantly slower global growth in the wake of the economic crisis, and slower growth translates into weaker demand for exports. Countries like South Africa that attracted short-term financial inflows are seeing these inflows fall off, as investors react to potential risk. South Africa used these inflows to finance consumption, and is now burdened with a large current account deficit that could trigger a currency crisis. It is clear that the macroeconomic liberalization policies implemented in the post-apartheid era have exposed the country to unstable global financial flows and built dependence on credit-driven consumption (*Mail & Guardian*, 2008). In the face of reduced capital inflows and slowed global growth, the size of the South African current account deficit is a threat to economic stability.

Many of the jobs that were created in South Africa are currently being lost, as consumption slows. Under crisis conditions – slowed growth, increasing unemployment, lower demand for exports, less foreign capital, lower consumption – one would expect that more workers will be pushed into street trading in the informal economy. Most traders working in the informal economy are there primarily because formal jobs are not available (Skinner, 2005). Fewer formal opportunities will likely mean more informal enterprises, but fewer customers.

This article is based on research carried out by the author, with 31 street traders in and around Johannesburg.[4] The research focused on street traders currently operating businesses, aiming to gain an understanding of the barriers they had encountered when going into trading, and challenges they were experiencing while trying to sustain their business in the face of the crisis. The field research was conducted in August 2008, at the start of the decline in retail sales as the crisis was being recognized. It used semi-structured interviews.

Of the 31 traders involved in the research, 12 were women and 19 were men (see Table 9.1). None of the trading businesses were registered to pay taxes. All were involved in selling new clothing. The motivation for selecting this particular group was, in part, that the sale of new clothing was likely to be more sensitive to changes in demand than trade in staple goods such as food. In addition, much of the clothing that traders sell is imported, and they therefore represent the distribution end of an international value chain that is serviced by the formal economy.

The 31 traders interviewed in my research had businesses ranging in age from less than one year to over 20 years. The average time of trading was eight years. It should be emphasized that this research was undertaken too early to capture the likely rise in informal trading as unemployed workers seek to survive. Anecdotal evidence suggests that this is happening (Timse, 2009).

Table 9.1 Trader demographics

	Immigrants (%)	South Africans (%)	Total (row %)
Male	14 (73.68)	5 (26.32)	19 (100.00)
Female	3 (25.00)	9 (75.00)	12 (100.00)
Total	17 (54.84)	14 (45.16)	31 (100.00)

Informal traders' motivations, start-up, and connections to the formal sector

In South Africa, lack of demand for labour by the formal economy has created a pool of unemployed people, some of whom see themselves as having no choice but to start a business in order to generate the income required to survive. One 22-year-old South African male trader said that he saw himself and other young people who are unemployed as having a choice only between starting a business and becoming criminals. He chose to start a business because the potential consequences of crime outweighed the appeal of immediate pay-off. Sixty per cent of all traders interviewed stated that they started their business primarily because of unemployment, and 40 per cent started primarily because they saw trading as a profitable opportunity. Men were more likely to report starting their businesses because they saw a profitable opportunity, while women were more likely to say they were motivated by unemployment.

It is important to note that *all* of the traders who identified unemployment as the primary reason for starting the business also saw it as a profitable opportunity. However, many of them qualified seeing a profitable opportunity with statements such as, 'it is more profitable than being unemployed'. When asked the question, 'What were your reasons for starting this business?', 17 of the 31 traders said they were unemployed, and several concluded their responses with statements like: 'it's better than nothing', 'I had no other choice', 'I couldn't find another job', 'Poverty' or 'There was no choice, my family was suffering in poverty'.

Most businesses were started with very little capital (the start-up cost for a trader selling new clothing ranged between R70 (US$25 at the 1991 exchange rate) and R6,000 for a business started in 2007 (US$851 at the 2007 exchange rate); the median was a little over US$100 in terms of the start-up years' exchange rates. Most had borrowed start-up money from family or friends, or used their own savings. Many people had begun by selling only a few things, or had started with low-cost items like cigarettes and sweets before moving into higher-profit items, such as shoes and clothing. When asked if he ever considered taking out a loan, one trader said yes, but that he had needed a bank account with money in it in order to get a loan – but if he had a bank account with money in it, then he wouldn't *need* a loan.[5]

Nearly all of the traders said they got supplies in bulk, but in small quantities, from formal shops that target traders as evidenced by painted signs stating 'hawkers welcome'. Another potential interaction with formal shops is through competition. Competition with formal shops was rarely cited as a challenge for traders when they were starting the business, but about 37 per cent now say that competition from formal shops is a problem. Traders who have businesses aged under three years are more likely to see formal shops as competition. Owners of businesses that are older are divided into half who say formal competition is a problem currently, and half who say it is not. I would speculate new shopping venues are the main reason, in addition to which it is probable that formal shops have become more of 'the norm' for some customers. This is fine. Women traders were more likely than men to see formal competition as a problem. It appears that female traders are more sensitive to changes in customers' behaviour and demand.

The next section discusses the impact of the crisis in terms of limited and falling consumer demand.

Demand-based constraints on street traders' businesses

Because the informal economy is intimately linked to the formal economy and macroeconomic conditions, when growth slows and unemployment increases, traders may see a decline in demand for their goods and services, and greater competition, leading to falling profits. Traders' own accounts suggest that this

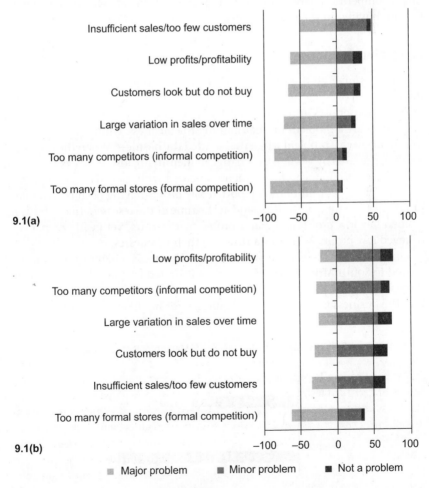

Figure 9.1 Current demand constraints (a) upon entry and (b) currently

is happening. The interview data suggest that female traders may be more sensitive to degraded demand conditions.

Seventy-five per cent of female traders, and 65 per cent of male traders, reported having made more money a year before the time of the research, which echoes a drop in consumer demand for retail goods (Statistics South Africa, 2009). The reason for fewer sales may be either lower demand by consumers, more competition from new traders, or a combination of both. As the number of traders increases, the number of customers would need to increase faster to keep profits from falling. While there was broad agreement among my research participants that sales are relatively slow, it is not possible definitively to separate the impact of a drop in market-wide consumption demand from the impact of competition.

Major problems most commonly identified by traders were low profits, too much competition, large variation in sales over time, and customers looking but not buying. In the next sections, I look more closely at each of these.

Profitability

Low profits may be the outcome of factors ranging from fewer customers, increased real or perceived competition, or additional pressure for income from growing households. Overall, about 80 per cent of respondents reported that low profits are a problem for maintaining the business, while 35 per cent said low profits were a problem when they started the business. When the responses are disaggregated by gender, the change in identifying low profits as a problem is especially pronounced for women compared with men. The same proportion, about 40 per cent of men reported low profits having been both a major problem at the time of start-up, and at the time of the research. In contrast, no women saw low profits as a major problem at start-up, yet nearly 85 per cent believed low profits were now a threat to their businesses.

One trader, a 32-year-old woman from Harare, Zimbabwe, said she had moved to South Africa to look for work, but started trading when she realized there were 'no jobs'. She has had her business for eight years, but is concerned that the business is earning too little money for her to keep it going.

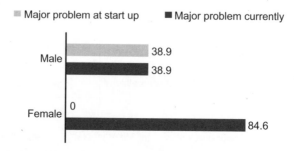

Figure 9.2 Percentage of traders identifying 'low profits' as a major problem

In general, the problem of low profits may reflect overtrading or market over-saturation. The more traders there are in the market, the lower demand is for each individual trader's goods. The data indicate that women's businesses tend to be more profitable than men's businesses.[6] Therefore, the gendered discrepancy between viewing low profits as a major problem does not reflect *actual* lower profits for women, but may instead reflect a greater sensitivity to low profits. This is explored in more detail in the following section.

Variable levels of trade

A second challenge is the fact that trade is not constant. There are specific times when sales are slow, and a few of the traders said they sometimes are unable to buy stock. While 25 per cent of respondents said that variable sales were a problem when they started their business, 75 per cent reported that unpredictable sales are a problem for maintaining the business now. Variable sales could become easier to contend with over time, as a trader learns the market patterns.

There was a gendered difference in traders reporting variable sales as a major problem, just as there had been regarding low profits.

The fact that variable levels of trade were reported as a major problem facing many of the traders – and in particular the female traders – may be due to the fact that nearly all of the traders interviewed are earning relatively low incomes all month or all year, and face a challenge to maintain their households. Even in relatively good times, making a living can be difficult if income is very low. During lulls, including those that are expected, hardship may result because saving income to smooth consumption is difficult or impossible when the business earnings tend to be low even when the business is relatively busy. As it is highly unlikely that female traders confront a more variable market than male traders, the data again indicate that female traders and their businesses may be more sensitive to variability. Several traders linked variability to inflation, which limits their customers spending on 'extras' like new sneakers or book-bags.

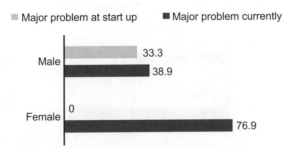

Figure 9.3 Percentage of traders identifying 'variable sales' as a major problem

Competition and over-trading

A third constraint is the ratio of buyers to sellers. Several traders pointed out that there are fewer customers because people are unemployed and are spending money only on necessities such as food and transportation. A rising number appear to be looking, but not ultimately buying.

While both male and female traders reported that there were fewer customers, female traders were far more likely to report that fewer customers, and customers looking but not buying, constitute major barriers to the sustainability of their businesses.

During the interviews, some of the traders suggested that an increase in the number of traders was responsible for a reduction in the number of customers per trader. Competition in the market is the single demand-based variable identified by both male and female traders far more frequently as a major problem currently than when they started the business.

A small proportion – 8 per cent of women and 6 per cent of men – reported that too many competitors posed them a major problem when they started trading. In comparison, over 75 per cent of women and 44 per cent of men now see too much competition as a major problem. Over 90 per cent

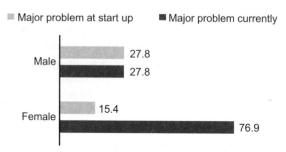

Figure 9.4 Percentage of traders identifying 'customers looking but not buying' as a major problem

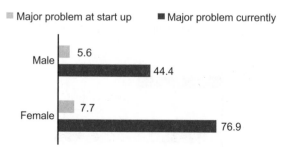

Figure 9.5 Percentage of traders identifying 'too many traders' as a major problem

of the traders interviewed said there are more traders now than there were one year ago.

Given that traders are setting prices and buying the same stock from the same suppliers, the perception of a highly competitive street trading environment seems to come from the insufficient number of customers and low profits. Competition manifests itself in a sense of insecurity and vulnerability shared by most of the traders, both male and female, but again, female traders are more likely to consider competition a major problem for their business.

Discussion of the findings

The survey data indicate that traders, particularly female traders, are sensitive to changes in demand and overtrading. Higher unemployment and lower demand, driven by the economic crisis, may constitute a disproportionate threat to the sustainability of women's trading businesses.

While demand and business income are perceived by the majority of traders of both genders to be lower than the year before, female traders are more likely to identify demand-based barriers such as low profits, customers looking but not buying and variable sales as major barriers to the sustainability of the business.

The finding that female traders are far more likely to view the demand barriers as major problems that they currently confront may be driven by several factors. The first and perhaps most important issue is that female traders' households appear to rely more heavily on income from the business than male traders' households.[7] The research findings suggest that female traders have lower household incomes than men, but slightly higher incomes from their businesses.

The reason that men report overall higher household incomes is because men are more likely to live in households with multiple income-earners. Sixty per cent of the women interviewed are the sole earner in their household, while this is true for only 32 per cent of men.

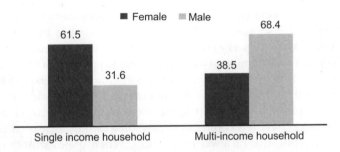

Figure 9.6 Percentage of female and male traders living in single- and multi-income households

The median household size of four does not vary by gender, but female traders' households are far more likely to be single-income households with more children. The eight female traders who were the single-income earner for their household supported 22 children in total, while of the six male single-income earners, five were supporting no children and one supported two children.

It seems likely, therefore, that female traders may be more sensitive to the constraints on customer demand for their goods, because their households rely more heavily on income from trading. The profit margin is so low that even predictable fluctuations in demand (and hence income) may prove problematic for women; particularly those who are sole income earners for their households.

A secondary, linked reason for traders to perceive business as comparatively unprofitable at the moment may be inflation. For most South Africans, the cost of basics such as food and transportation has risen, and households may have an increasingly difficult time making ends meet. However, more research would be needed, with a larger sample, and questions focusing specifically on household vulnerability, in order to draw more concrete conclusions about the gendered perception of demand-based constraints.

Conclusions

The people who are currently losing their jobs in the formal sector, as well as others who work informally, for example as cleaners, are street traders' customers. The informal economy, and trading in particular, may act at first as a fall-back income-generating option for the unemployed, but this means more competition. Before the economic crisis, there was very high unemployment, and the informal economy was already crowded relative to the level of customer demand for the products and services on offer. The informal sector is unlikely to be able to absorb more workers, be they newly retrenched or new entrants into the labour force. Slower growth, fewer jobs, less disposable income, and more competition all result in lower income for traders, already a vulnerable group.

For the traders that I interviewed, the primary effects of the economic crisis are lower profits and greater competition. All traders are vulnerable, but female traders are especially insecure; most are already earning incomes that are insufficient for supporting a household, reinvesting in their business or saving money. Many traders were barely able to eke out a subsistence living for themselves and their families. One woman was supporting her four children on her income from trading and Child Support Grants of R460 (US$46 at the time) per month and her situation was not unusual. The income generated by trading has not been high in the past, but the current crisis is exacerbating the problem. Traders have few coping strategies; they cannot increase their hours due to safety concerns, or lower their prices. When their earnings decrease because of external forces, they have no business-based way to respond. Female traders and their households seem to suffer the most, because their households are more reliant on income from trading.

The Bree Street traders in my research have had no involvement in the construction of the New Financial Architecture; and they have been largely excluded from the social groups worldwide who have benefited from it. However, they are one of many marginalized groups who will bear the damage of its collapse.

Notes

1. There are some known problems with the LFS data, which may result in under-counting informal activity (see Devey et al., [2003] and Webster et al., [2008] for more information on problems with the LFS). However, these data are the best available at a national level.
2. The official unemployment rate includes 3,945,000 '[p]ersons aged 15–65 who did not have a job or business in the seven days prior to the survey interview but had looked for work or taken steps to start a business in the four weeks prior to the interview and were available to take up work within two weeks of the interview' (Statistics South Africa, 2007: 210).
3. The expanded definition here includes those classified as officially unemployed, and 3,425,000 'discouraged work-seekers', defined as '[p]ersons who want to work and are available to work but who say that they are not actively looking for work' (Statistics South Africa, 2007: 210).
4. The research was carried out by the author under the Corporate Strategy and Industrial Development Research Programme (CSID) at the University of the Witwatersrand, Johannesburg, South Africa. The Office of the South African Presidency provided the funding for the field research discussed in this article, through its Second Economy Strategies Project, administered by the Trade and Industrial Policy Strategies (TIPS). The project is part of the author's dissertation research for a PhD in the Department of Economics at the University of Massachusetts in Amherst, MA, USA.
5. Most traders were unwilling to take loans from banks, in part because they felt that their businesses are vulnerable and loans were too risky. See also Cichello (2005).
6. The median monthly business income for a female trader was R1,200 (US$120 at the time of the interview), while for male traders the median was R1,000 (US$100 at the time of the interview).
7. The income data are to be treated with caution, as some traders were unable or unwilling to disclose earnings.

Bibliography

Chen, M. (2007) 'Rethinking the informal economy: linkages with the formal economy and the formal regulatory environment', United Nations

Department of Economic and Social Affairs (DESA) Working Paper no. 46, www.un.org/esa/desa/papers/2007/wp46_2007.pdf (last accessed 28 April 2010).

Cichello, P. (2005) 'Hindrances to self-employment activity: evidence from the 2000 Khayelitsha/Mitchell's plain survey', Center for Social Science Research Working Paper no. 131:58, www.sarpn.org.za/documents/d0001752/index. php (last accessed 28 April 2010).

Crotty, J. (2009) 'Structural causes of the global financial crisis: a critical assessment of the "new financial architecture"', *Cambridge Journal of Economics* 33:4, pp. 563–580.

Devey, R., Skinner, C. and Valodia, I. (2003) 'Informal economy employment data in South Africa: a critical analysis', paper presented at TIPS and DPRU Forum 2003, 8–10 September 2003, Johannesburg, South Africa, www. inclusivecities.org/pdfs/devey%20skinner%20valodia%20Informal%20 Economy%20employment%20data%20in%20ZA.pdf (last accessed 28 April 2010).

Fisher, S. (1998) 'Capital account liberalization and the role of the IMF', *Should the IMF Pursue Capital-Account Convertibility? Essays in International Finance*, No. 207, International Finance Section, Department of Economics, Princeton University, www.princeton.edu/~ies/IES_Essays/E207.pdf (last accessed 28 April 2010).

Hart, K. (1976) 'The politics of unemployment in Ghana', *African Affairs*, 75:301, pp. 488–497.

IMF (2008) 'South Africa: financial system stability assessment', IMF Country Report no. 08/349, www.imf.org/external/pubs/ft/scr/2008/cr08349.pdf (last accessed 28 April 2010).

Mail & Guardian (2008) 'Manuel: SA "reasonably iinsulated" from financial storm', *Mail & Guardian*, 10 October, www.mg.co.za/article/2008-10-10-manuel-sa-reasonably-insulated-from-financial-storm (last accessed 28 April 2010).

Mbeki, T. (2003) 'Letter from the President: bold steps to end the "two nations" divide', *ANC Today*, 3(33), 22–28 August, www.anc.org.za/ancdocs/anctoday/2003/at33.htm (last accessed 28 April 2010).

Peterson, V.S. (2003) *A Critical Rewriting of Global Political Economy: Integrating Reproductive, Productive, and Virtual Economies*, Routledge, London.

Reynolds, N. and van Zyl, J. (2006) *South Africa's 'Dual Economy'*, South African New Economics Network www.sane.org.za/docs/views/showviews. asp?ID=174 (last accessed 28 April 2010).

Skinner, C. (2005) 'Constraints to growth and employment in Durban: evidence from the informal economy', Working Paper no. 65, http://sds.ukzn.ac.za/ default.php? 7,6,154,4,0l (last accessed 28 April 2010).

Statistics South Africa (2007) *Labour Force Survey*, Statistical Release no. P0210.

Statistics South Africa (2009) *Retail Trade Sales*, Statistical Release no. P6242.1.

Timse, T. (2009) 'Unemployment forces many to street trading', *Mail & Guardian*, 2 August, www.mg.co.za/article/2009-08-02-unemployment-forces-many-to-street-trading (last accessed 28 April 2010).

Velia, M., Valodia, I. and Amisi, B. (2006) 'Trade dynamics in used clothing: the case of Durban, South Africa', Research Report, 71, School of Development Studies, University of KwaZulu-Natal Durban, South Africa, http://sds.ukzn.ac.za/files/RR71%20Velia.pdf (last accessed 7 June 2010).

Webster, E., Benya, A., Dilata, X., Joynt, K., Ngoepe, K. and Tsoeu, M. (2008) 'Making visible the invisible: confronting South Africa's decent work deficit', Report for the Department of Labour, www.labour.gov.za/documents/research-documents/making-visible-the-invisible-confronting-south-africa2019s-decent-work-deficit (last accessed 28 April 2010).

World Bank (2002) 'South Africa: constraints to growth in Johannesburg's black informal sector: evidence from the 1999 informal sector survey', Report No. 24449-ZA [obtained from Task Team leader Vandana Chandra].

World Bank (2008) 'Global financial crisis and implications for developing countries', background paper from the G-20 Finance Ministers' Meeting, 8 November, Sao Paulo, Brazil, www.worldbank.org/financialcrisis/pdf/G20FinBackgroundpaper.pdf (last accessed 28 April 2010).

About the author

Jennifer Cohen is a PhD Candidate at the Department of Economics, University of Massachusetts. The field research cited in the chapter was undertaken while she was a Senior Researcher with the Corporate Strategy and Industrial Development Research Programme, University of the Witwatersrand, Johannesburg, South Africa.

CHAPTER 10

Crisis, care and childhood: the impact of economic crisis on care work in poor households in the developing world

Jessica Espey, Caroline Harper and Nicola Jones

This chapter first appeared in *Gender & Development* 18(2), pp. 291–307, July 2010.

Caring for children and other dependents is crucial to human well-being, and to social and economic development. Yet, most national and international policymakers appear persistently blind to this fact, as has been highlighted by the recent global economic crisis. They need to recognize and value care work if they are to support vulnerable families from the effects of economic downturn. The 2008–2009 global economic crisis has served to underscore the potential effects of inadequate attention to care economy dynamics, with serious risks to children's education, development, health and protection already evident. Nevertheless, economic recovery measures continue to provide little space or funding for protective or remedial measures. We argue that gender and care-sensitive social protection measures are a good means by which to support the position of carers and to create better visibility within policy circles, while also demonstrating considerable returns for human well-being and broader long-term economic development. These returns are evident in pre-existing social protection programmes, from which it will be vital to learn lessons. Including care-sensitive social protection in economic recovery packages also has the potential to improve the visibility and importance of care in a transformative and sustainable way.

Introduction

Currently, many developing countries are experiencing the impact of the global economic crisis. Its effects include mass unemployment, with workers being laid off from formal work within sectors which are directly linked to global markets, declining remittance flows, and a reduction in government spending on social services, owing to fiscal constraints. These effects are having an impact on family life, as breadwinners have to work longer days or take on additional employment to earn sufficient for survival. This leads to them having less time to care for their families. Older children are being withdrawn from school to save fees, or pulled out of school to provide substitute care for younger siblings; there is less food to eat and it is lower quality, and spending on other household necessities is also reduced. Families and individuals are finding themselves increasingly dependent on (often-depleted) community resources. As this article argues, all of these effects have considerable ramifications for the well-being of children and their carers (Harper et al., forthcoming).

This chapter starts by providing a brief overview of how academic and advocacy work has treated the issue of domestic care (focusing predominantly upon unpaid childcare). Turning then to the economic crisis, we examine the ways in which the economic crisis is affecting care for children in poor households. Drawing on evidence from past crises also, we aim to highlight the ways in which households are responding to the crisis and to identify the extent to which their coping efforts are supported by the state and their communities through formal and informal methods. Such safety net measures are often referred to as 'social protection'. In the final section, we discuss the implications for policymakers facing the current crisis that emerge from lessons learned in past crises.

The economics of care

Over the past four decades, many feminist economists have highlighted the importance of investing in childcare, for economic dynamism and growth. The United Nations Development Fund for Women (UNIFEM) and United Nations Research Institute for Social Development (UNRISD), in particular, have highlighted women's care-related contribution to the economy – through time-use studies, and by costing the impact and contribution of unpaid care work to gross domestic product (Budlender, 2007). An understanding of the importance of the 'care economy' is gradually being adopted by mainstream economists. Recent work by the Nobel Prize-winning economist James Heckman has studied and argued for the positive economic returns of investments in childcare. James Heckman argues that there may be costly state-funded interventions required in later life, if a child's physical or mental health is impaired (Heckman, 2006). Children deprived of good care are more likely to become involved in crime as adults, and to earn less, than children who have received good care (Heckman and Masterov, 2007). Heckman's argument that governments which invest in and support early childhood development reap the benefits through increased productivity later in the life cycle is also advanced by economic institutions, including the World Bank (Hanushek and Wobmann, 2007). These views support a growing consensus that investments in different dimensions of child well-being, (aiming to improve cognitive skills, behaviour, and health), are interlinked in important ways, and mutually reinforcing.

Given the steadily increasing recognition of the importance of care work within development policy arenas, one might expect policy responses to the current global economic crisis to be sensitive to the fact that many poor households struggle to meet the needs of children for care – referred to in policy circles as the 'burden of care'. Yet, for the most part, these issues have been largely absent from policy agendas.

Studies examining household time-use and the differences in women's and men's household responsibilities, and paid and unpaid employment, have shown how urgent it is for policy and programming to improve with regard to childcare. Time-use studies such as that by ECLAC (2007) in Latin America have demonstrated that men and women have very different levels of input into care work in the home. In Brazil, 90 per cent of women spend an average of 20 hours per week on unpaid domestic chores, while only 45 per cent of men do such work, averaging just seven hours per week.

In South Africa, a study by Kizilirmak and Memis (2009) has gone further, demonstrating not only women's disproportionate burden of care for dependents within the home, but also the correlation between household responsibilities and poverty. They found that for women, household responsibilities and care burdens intensify in accordance with the depth of their poverty. In contrast, for the men in their sample, growing poverty did not mean that men spent more time doing unpaid work. In fact, poverty had no direct correlation to the amount of time that men in this study spent doing unpaid work.

These surveys have reinforced the argument that policymakers need to recognize the essential nature of the social (and economic) services provided by women; the lack of support within their communities and from the state; and the necessity for better recognition of the correlation between gendered experiences of poverty, and women's disproportionate responsibility to provide care for dependents.

Jody Heymann, in her seminal work *Forgotten Families* (Heymann, 2008), highlights the ways in which policymakers fail to consider the nature and importance of the care economy. Specifically, she identifies the strong correlation between the global economic system and the position of unpaid carers in the developing world. Processes of industrialization and urbanization in the emerging and developing world are resulting in a steady increase in demand for a large, inexpensive labour-force, and the tendency for nuclear families to migrate in search of new job opportunities tied to global industrial markets, leaving their extended family – and the support it gave them to care for their dependents – far behind. These new job opportunities seldom offer any form of support for care of children (and other dependents), rarely have adequate social legislation or benefits, and in the developing world are often compounded by being informal, subject to long hours and poor pay.

Heymann cites evidence from a study of working families in countries undergoing major socioeconomic transitions, such as Botswana, Mexico and Viet Nam. In half of the families in Botswana, over one-third of the families in Mexico, and one-fifth of the families in Viet Nam, children are left home alone on a regular or occasional basis. Moreover, 52 per cent of families leaving children home alone relied on other children to help with childcare. Jody Heymann and her co-author Monica Ruis-Casares conclude that: 'poverty, social integration, local norms, and child development frame parents' decisions regarding care. Insufficient societal support to working families frequently resulted in unsafe childcare arrangements and limited parental involvement in child education and health care' (Ruiz-Casares and Heymann, 2009: 312). The conclusions emphasize that such problems cannot be dismissed simply as problems of parental neglect; they are also problems of communal and societal neglect by policymakers who need to widen their frame of vision.

The impact of the economic crisis upon care

The relationship between the global economy, employment opportunities in the developing world, and the impact of this employment upon childcare has become much more evident with the onset of the global economic crisis. Recent research by the Overseas Development Institute (ODI) for the United Nations Children's Fund (UNICEF) has sought to investigate household coping strategies in the face of complex economic crises, the effects upon children and women living in or with the potential to descend into poverty, and the extent to which different economic and social measures have mitigated the effects. This body of work has identified the considerable impact upon the care and well-being of children, confirming the connections between the household and the global economy (Harper et al., forthcoming).

Connections between the crisis and household care

For some developing countries, the impact of the recent global economic crisis is mostly being felt through declining remittance flows, while for others, levels of trade or exchange rates have been volatile. In still other countries, the crisis may be most potently felt through declines in international aid. Importantly, though, for many poor households, the implications of these negative macroeconomic effects on the lives of real women and men – for example on their employment, household income, public service availability, household responsibilities and ability to provide adequate care for dependents – are similar.

Figure 10.1 shows the macroeconomic dimensions of the crisis: reduced financial flows, remittances, trade and prices, and aid, and their effects at country level. These effects vary according to local contexts and conditions. The second tier presents potential meso-level effects which may include declining investment in public services, higher unemployment, diminished consumption capacity, and reduced access to credit. The third tier then depicts the ways in which governmental policy responses shape households' ability to function, which in turn may translate into children's experiences of multidimensional poverty. Identifying the scale and duration of these potential

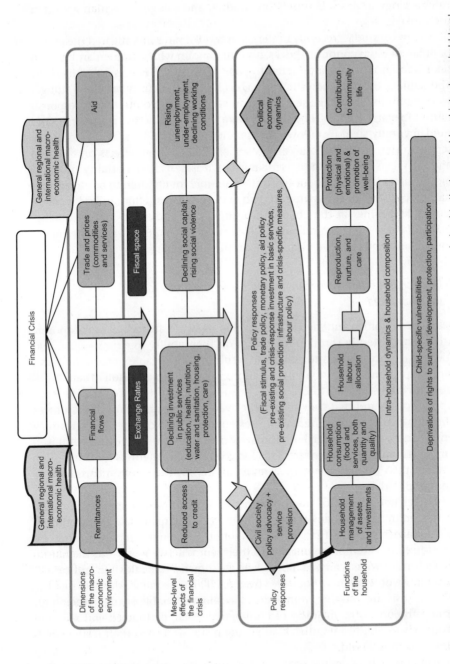

Figure 10.1 The transmission mechanisms of the global economic crisis from the macroeconomic level to the household and intra-household level
Source: Harper et al. (forthcoming).

effects at each level is clearly important. Experience from previous crises indicates a range of possible effects on children and caregivers, which are often interlinked.

A range of studies recently undertaken by ODI have investigated the effects of different past economic shocks, and the ways in which women and men in poor households have attempted to cope with these.[1] Effects on individuals and families include poorer nutrition, declining attendance at school, longer working hours, and increased strains on adults trying to meet their responsibilities for family care. These effects were discernible across continents, and fundamentally stem from lower household income, and less access to public services (Marcus, 2009; Jones and Marsden, 2009). Other effects on children and caregivers in some contexts included increases in child mortality and morbidity, increased child labour (with the potential for children to be engaged in hazardous forms of employment), and violence against children and women, alongside declines in the quality of nurture, care and emotional well-being. Many of these effects could have long-term implications, over the lifetime of individuals, and may even impact upon the next generation.

Impact on households, responses and the implications for the care of children

Many poor women and men in the developing world are feeling the economic crisis most potently through its impact on their ability to earn income, and increasing prices, which together can result in considerable household stress. Unemployment and an inability to afford necessities may require that household members take on more time-consuming and often poorer-paid work opportunities and that they have to be even leaner with what little resources they have, thereby cutting back on essentials. These coping strategies may ensure short-term survival, but ultimately may compromise the long-term welfare of all household members. This focus on the short-term is nowhere more evident than in relation to the care of children, which is often considerably compromised.

The characteristics of unemployment vary, but are commonly strongly patterned by age, gender, ethnicity and location (Harper et al., forthcoming). The evidence suggests that women are often disproportionately affected by crisis-induced unemployment due to their reproductive work, and the nature of their paid work, which is more likely than men's to be flexible and casual, rendering women more vulnerable (Truong, 2000). Emerging evidence from the current crisis suggests that women are especially vulnerable owing to their high concentration in the majority of temporary, casual, contracted and seasonal work, where significant cutbacks are being made, as well as their responsibilities in the household.[2]

Demands on women's time tend to increase under conditions of economic crisis, heightened unemployment, and deepening household poverty

(Antonopoulos, 2008). For example, in Argentina, where employment of women increased from 2002 during the Convertibility Crisis, there remained little change in women's domestic responsibilities (MacDonald et al., 2005), ultimately decreasing the time they could spend on care and nurture. If parents in this position cannot call on formal social services, elderly people or older children may have to fill the gap, which can often result in compromises in older children's schooling (United Nations Development Programme [UNDP], 2009). If these options are unavailable, children may have to be left at home alone. Although quantitative evidence relating to hours of care is hard to come by, Ruiz-Casares and Heymann's (2009) study of child neglect in Botswana, Mexico and Viet Nam has highlighted that the problem of insufficient childcare is most acute in countries with limited support networks, an inability to afford childcare and intensifying labour hours.

Households facing crisis are also often forced to cut back on spending – first on non-essentials and then on essentials. This is clearly a short-term unsustainable strategy with serious impact on health and well-being. In this current crisis, there is already evidence of poorer quantity and quality of food intake among poor families in Bangladesh, Indonesia, Jamaica, Kenya and Zambia (Hossain et al., 2009), owing to lower household income, local currency depreciations and/or food price hikes. Women often act as 'shock absorbers' of household food insecurity, reducing their own consumption despite increased maternal wasting and anaemia, and effects on infant health (Block et al., 2004; Quisumbing et al., 2008, cited in Holmes et al., 2009).

Families may well be forced to cut back on visiting health facilities, with impact on children's health. For instance, in East Asia, during the 1997–1998 financial crisis, there was a decline in the use of child health services (for example, by 10 per cent in Indonesia, and 8.5 per cent in Korea), with the exception of Thailand, where private service usage resulted in a significant shift towards poorer-quality public services (Jones and Marsden, forthcoming).[3]

People's mental health and well-being suffers as a result of stress. In Indonesia, Thailand and South Korea, following the 1997 East Asian financial crisis, there were reported increases in psychological distress among both male and female adults, owing to unemployment and financial instability (Friedman and Thomas 2007). This is not only an issue for adults, but also for the children who depend on them (Conger et al., 1992; Kahn et al., 2004).[4] Violence may increase in the household too. In Thailand, during 1997/1998 (Knowles et al., 1999), for instance, domestic violence increased, and in itself was found to be a common cause of stress among women (Lotrakul, 2006). Similar reports of increased domestic violence have also come from Indonesia (Suharto, 2007), Malaysia (Knowles et al., 1999), and Korea (ibid.). Violence of this nature, and particularly that inflicted upon children, is in general poorly reported and what information there is tends not to be captured in national data, but rather elicited through qualitative research. However, the decline in the quality of nurture, care and protection owing to psychological ill-health has widespread consequences for children's development (Harper et al., forthcoming).

Community-level responses and the importance of social networks

Communities can work together to help families and individuals weather hard times, and can be pivotal for the care of children. Social networks – of family, neighbours and friends – represent a crucial asset. However, these are also susceptible to the effects of crisis. When people are consistently subject to a certain level of acute poverty, fostering relationships which depend on reciprocal giving can become very difficult.

In Latin America, during a period of austerity brought on by economic structural adjustment policies implemented in the 1980s and early 1990s, community soup kitchens helped families secure enough food, and shored up community support (Burt, 1997). In Lima's *barriadas* (suburban squatter settlements), the 'glass of milk' programmes sought to encourage the formation of grassroots groups (ibid.). These initiatives not only enabled families to stave off severe malnutrition, but also brought people together in the midst of acute economic strain, thereby fostering social networks and community participation as well as providing some persons with administrative skills.

Nevertheless, as the period of economic structural adjustment crisis continued into the 1990s, many organizations – particularly the Peruvian soup kitchens – became increasingly dependent upon external donors, and contributions from their membership. Many poor families were no longer able to participate, since they could not afford even a small membership contribution.[5] Similarly the strains of administering these community mechanisms became evident in heightened corruption, conflict over the way resources were administrated, and power struggles (Delpino, 1991, cited in Burt, 1997). In Kyrgyzstan, during the economic crisis induced by transition, it was noted that while poor people rely heavily on their social networks, these have tended to become more 'horizontal' (that is, mostly consisting of other poor people) as the lives of poor and better-off people have diverged. As a result, the help these networks can provide is limited – mostly food and second-hand clothes (Ablezova et al., 2004), with poor households becoming increasingly isolated (Harper et al., forthcoming).

Mitigating the impact: counter-cyclical spending and transformative social protection

There is widespread acknowledgement that one way in which countries can mitigate the impact of the economic crisis is through 'counter-cyclical spending' (that is, by increasing investment in social services and social protection during a downturn, to cushion vulnerable population groups from the effects of negative economic cycles). The wisdom is that this will not only support those made most vulnerable by the crisis, but will, in the long term, give the best economic and social returns (Sánchez and Vos 2009). However, in developing countries there is widespread debate about how to manage this. Such an approach requires innovative financing (possibly supported by international transfers) to balance budgets, yet manage the threat of becoming dependent on aid in the long term.[6]

Economic stimulus packages (ESPs) are financial investments intended to create jobs and promote investment and consumer spending during an economic downturn or recession. They are going some way to ensure that recovery efforts not only support financial markets, but also provide social services and social investments. According to a study by UNIFEM (2009), the majority of Asian ESPs, such as those in Korea, Malaysia and the Philippines, include investments in basic services such as health care, education, and sanitation. These investments will allow the poor continued access to essential services.

ESPs and wider policy responses to the economic crisis can mitigate the impact upon households in a potentially gender and care-sensitive manner, through a variety of social protection measures. Social protection can be defined as public actions which are designed to reduce poverty, vulnerability and risk throughout the lifecycle. Such actions seek to provide protection from adversity (for example, from loss of employment or natural disasters), to prevent harmful coping responses (such as selling assets, or resorting to the use of child labour), to promote ways out of poverty and vulnerability by encouraging investments in people's knowledge or skills, supporting new income-generating opportunities, and transforming social relations through anti-discrimination measures.

The policies and programmes included in social protection involve four major kinds of activities: social insurance programmes (for example, pensions, or publicly provided health insurance); social assistance (for example, school feeding programmes, which enable children to keep attending school during economic shocks, 'food for work' schemes, cash or in-kind transfers); social welfare services (services for people who need special care, for instance, people living with disabilities, orphans, refugees); and social equity measures (for example, anti-discrimination legislation, or family violence prevention legislation) (Devereux and Sabates-Wheeler, 2004). Recent reviews suggest that the efficacy of such programmes has been limited by poor attention to issues of gender and age inequalities (Kabeer, 2008), but there are a variety of cost-effective measures which can be adopted to help strengthen the role that social protection plays in supporting the maintenance of the care economy in times of crisis (Holmes and Jones, 2009b).

Nonetheless, to date, crisis-specific social protection responses have been relatively limited (McCord and Vandermootele, 2009) and there are still considerable limitations with the coverage and infrastructure of pre-existing systems. For instance, many people are employed in informal labour markets and, therefore, it is hard to identify those households out of work (Harper et al., forthcoming). Nevertheless there remains momentum and opportunity for transformative action, as demonstrated at the London Summit 2009 where the G20 pledged not only to stabilize the global financial system, but to provide US$50 billion to support social protection, boost trade and safeguard development in low income countries (The London Summit, 2009).

There is much that can be learned across countries and from past social protection programmes to ensure that responses to the current economic crisis are sensitive to both gender and care dynamics, and take into account children's longer-term development and well-being. In developed countries, attempts to implement child-sensitive social protection measures have tended to focus upon forms of caregivers' allowances or citizens' wages, taxation allowances, different types of paid and unpaid leave from employment, social security credits and social services. In developing countries, with newly emerging or scanty welfare systems, these mechanisms tend to be bundled into broader discussions around promoting food security, agricultural productivity, supporting income generation activities and enhancing human capital, but with little attention to gender and care (Holmes and Jones, 2009a). However, this is not to say that there are not transferable lessons and replicable strategies.

A key hindrance to the effective consideration of care dynamics is the focus of ESP resources on infrastructure and public works. Although these may have benefits for women and their dependents by providing a practical response to families facing a short-term drop in income or by tiding them over potentially 'hungry' periods of the year, the primary beneficiaries are likely to be men, who typically do not shoulder domestic and care work responsibilities and are often more physically suited to the hard physical labour that many public works schemes require. Moreover, although there are few assessments of both the gender and care sensitivity of most public works programmes, what analysis there is suggests that only a limited number incorporate care-sensitive considerations into their design (Quisumbing et al., 2008). In general, few mechanisms are provided for women to participate on a flexible basis: the actual labour undertaken often imposes heavier time and effort costs on poor women, who are typically already overworked, than on poor men (Devereux, 2002); women may be pressured by men not to compete for traditionally male dominated jobs; and finally the design of many public works programmes suffer from the absence of women in decision-making structures (Holmes and Jones, 2009a).

Some schemes have, however, benefited from efforts to demonstrate gender-sensitivity, in some instances making explicit provisos for the care of children; for example, in Botswana's Labour-Intensive Rural Public Works Programme and Ethiopia's Productive Safety Net Programme (PSNP), women are given time off for pregnancy and for breast-feeding. Both the PSNP in Ethiopia and India's National Rural Employment Guarantee Scheme (NREGS) have specifically included the provision of childcare facilities or crèches in their programme design. The PSNP also allows for flexibility in terms of women's working hours, so they can balance domestic responsibilities including the care of children (Holmes and Jones, 2009a). Positive consideration could also be given to the expansion of public works programmes to include social sector activities that not only use more labour and fewer machines, or tools, but are also well-suited to 'unskilled' women workers, who are already carrying out such work on an unpaid basis in their homes (Antonpolous, 2007).

Alternatively, a form of social protection which arguably better supports a child's long-term development is to provide financial recognition for childcare. This not only frees up pressures on care time, but additionally provides a source of income. Caregiver allowances, such as the child grant in South Africa[7] have demonstrated considerable success as they not only recognize the economic value of household care work but may incentivize families to provide better care. In South Africa the child support grant is a means-tested grant awarded to the primary caregivers of poor children under the age of seven (Lund, 2002). It has demonstrated effective range and depth of coverage, and has had noticeably positive effects upon children's care; in particular, improving child health.

For older or school-age children, social protection can be oriented around the educational setting, maintaining and improving attendance even in the context of economic crisis. School feeding programmes can provide a relatively large proportion of daily calorie, protein and other nutrient requirements. In some countries, eligibility is universal. The Brazilian Constitution of 1988, for example, specifically states that school feeding is a universal right of all school-age children. However, in other countries, for example Bangladesh, geographic or other targeting of schools or individuals is undertaken (FAO, 2001). Chile's school feeding programme successfully targets the lowest-income quintiles, and provides a strong incentive for parents to send their children to school: 58 per cent of the children in rural areas completed primary education in 1990, compared with only 40 per cent in 1986 (FAO, 2001; Kain, 2002).

If social welfare services aiming to protect children are co-ordinated with broader social protection systems (Jones, 2009), this can respond to the problem of domestic violence and child neglect. In a recent study of West African social protection mechanisms (Jones, 2009), a number of strategies were identified which can achieve this. These include, for example, building the capacity of government ministries which manage social protection transfers and core social services (including protective services for children), to enhance the efficiency of cross-referrals, and to develop common data systems to monitor better the well-being of vulnerable children. Another strategy identified was to strengthen legislation to support children's protection from abuse and neglect.

Most important is building comprehensive systems for monitoring and evaluation into social protection, so that commitments made to provide care services or to take into account gender dynamics and ensure equal opportunities are upheld and executed effectively. It is also vital that a transformative approach is taken in the design of social protection programmes. Indeed, as

Antonopoulos (2007) has highlighted in her critique of public works, it is not enough to consider the practical limitations, like a lack of crèche facilities, if there is still no recognition of the value of, nor any attempt to redistribute the costs of, intra-household care.

Conclusion

Economic crises past and present underscore the way in which childcare (largely unpaid, and performed by women), is the bedrock of a functioning economy, and an integral part of human well-being. Compromising the level or quality of care that a child receives can have considerable implications for long-term development and economic productivity. Adequate consideration of these dynamics and effective mechanisms to support women's productive employment, without compromising the care of their children, is therefore essential.

Social protection that adequately captures both economic and social risks, and pays heed to the value of childcare (enabling women and men to earn income while also enabling them to care for, nurture and protect children), is a viable and durable means of integrating a care-sensitive approach within social safety nets and national welfare systems. Sharing past lessons, like those described herein will be vital for the improvement and greater efficacy of social protection systems. If integrated into economic crisis policy responses these measures may help to safeguard against future shocks and to also improve pre-existing childcare and gender-related vulnerabilities. Implementing gender- and care-sensitive social protection also presents an opportunity to demonstrate a considerable shift in both our perceptions and appreciation of the care economy.

Notes

1. The 2009/2010 ODI/UNICEF study consisted of four papers examining a wide variety of past macroeconomic shocks and their impacts upon households and children. The regional papers focused upon Latin America (the Mexican Peso Crises of 2002 and the Argentinean convertibility crisis); the impact of transition upon post Soviet states (with a focus upon Kyrgyzstan); the East Asian financial crisis of 1997; and the impact of commodity price fluctuations within Africa since the 1990s. A summary synthesis paper was prepared for a conference on Children and Crisis in November 2009 (held at UNICEF London); see Harper et al. (forthcoming).
2. See Dejardin and Owens (2009) and Sirimanne (2009) on this and for policy options for engendering macroeconomic and social protection responses.
3. During the East Asian financial crisis the proportion of household income spent on food rose disproportionately (particularly in urban areas). In

Indonesia the proportion of households spending more than 65 per cent of total expenditure on food more than doubled in urban areas between February 1997 and February 1999, from 18 per cent to 39 per cent (Dhanani and Islam, 2002).

4. Kahn et al. (2004) found that the impacts of mental health symptoms among parents on the emotional and behavioural well-being of their children included 'external' indicators, such as: sudden changes in mood or feeling; disobedience; nervousness; trouble getting along with other children; restless or over-active behaviour, and 'internal' indicators, including: feelings of worthlessness and inferiority; unhappiness and sadness; fearfulness and anxiousness; and being easily confused. These impacts intensified if a child had two parents with psychological problems.

5. As with the soup kitchens in Latin America, in Kyrgyzstan, evidence from the late 1990s found poor people increasingly unable to afford even the modest cash contributions needed to participate in rotational savings clubs (Kuehnast and Dudwick, 2002).

6. A detailed discussion on the appropriateness of counter-cyclical investments within low-income countries was recently aired at the 2009 PEGnet conference (Policies for Reducing Inequality in the Developing World) at the Hague. See www.pegnet.ifw-kiel.de/.

7. South Africa has been a beacon in its recognition and value of care, not only implementing a caregiver allowance, but additionally implementing a comprehensive national-level capacity development programme: the Early Child Development Programme (part of the Expanded Public Works Programme, set up in 2004). The ambitions of this programme are to improve national childcare systems, to provide employment opportunities for women and promote the professional development of women working in the childcare field. The programme 'can free parents and other adult carers to take up opportunities for education and employment' (Department of Social Development, 2006; 12 quoted in Lund, [2009]).

Bibliography

Ablezova, M., Botoeva, G., Jukusheva, T., Marcus, R. and Satybaldieva, E. (2004) 'A generation at risk? Childhood poverty in Kyrgyzstan', CHIP Report 15, Childhood Poverty Research and Policy Centre, London.

ADB (2003) *Social Protection: Policies and Strategie*, Asian Development Bank, Manila, Philippines.

Aguero, J.M., Carter, M.R. and Woolard, I. (2007) 'The impact of unconditional cash transfers on nutrition: the South African child support grant', International Poverty Centre Working Paper no. 39.

Antonopoulos, R. (2007) 'The right to a job, the right types of projects: employment guarantee policies from a gender perspective', Working Paper no. 516, The Levy Economics Institute, New York.

Antonopoulos, R. (2008) 'The unpaid care work–paid work connection', Working Paper no. 541, The Levy Institute of Bard College, New York.

Antonopoulos, R. (2009) 'The current economic and financial crisis: a gender perspective', Working Paper no. 562, The Levy Economic Institute of Bard College, New York.

Block, S.A., Kiess, L., Webb, P., Kosen, S., Moench-Pfanner, R., Bloem, M. and Timmer, C.P. (2004) 'Macro shocks and micro outcomes: child nutrition during Indonesia's crisis', *Economics and Human Biology* 2:1, pp. 21–44.

Budlender, D. (2007) 'A critical review of selected time use surveys', Political and Social Economy of Care Series, Paper no. 2, Gender and Development Research Programme, UNRISD, Geneva, Switzerland.

Burt, J.M. (1997) 'Political violence and the grassroots in Lima, Peru', in D.A. Chalmers et al. (ed.) *The New Politics of Inequality in Latin America: Rethinking Participation and Representation*, Oxford University Press, Oxford, UK.

Case, A., Hosegood, V. and Lund, F. (2003) 'The reach of the South African child support grant: evidence from KwaZulu-Natal', Working Paper 38, Centre for Social and Development Studies, University of Natal, Durban, South Africa.

Conger, R.D., Conger, K.J., Elder, G.H., Lorenz, F.O., Simons, R.L. and Whitbeck, L.B. (1992) 'Family process model of economic hardship and adjustment of early adolescent boys', *Child Development* 63:3, pp. 526–541.

Davies, M. and McGregor, J.A. (2009) 'Social protection responses to the financial crisis: what do we know?', IDS In Focus Policy Briefing 7, IDS, Brighton, UK.

Dejardin, A.K. and Owens, J. (2009) 'Asia in the global economic crisis: impacts and responses from a gender perspective', technical note for meeting: responding to the Economic Crisis – Coherent Policies for Growth, Employment and Decent Work in Asia and Pacific, Manila, Philippines, 18–20 February 2009.

Devereux, S. (2002) 'From workfare to fair work. The contribution of public works and other labour-based infrastructure programmes to poverty alleviation', Issues in Employment and Poverty Discussion Paper 5, ILO, Geneva, Switzerland.

Devereux, S. and Sabates-Wheeler, R. (2004) 'Transformative social protection', Working Paper 232, Institute of Development Studies, Brighton.

Dhanani, S. and Islam, I. (2002) 'Poverty, vulnerability and social protection in a period of crisis: the case of Indonesia', *World Development* 30:7, pp. 1211–1231.

Economic Commission for Latin America and the Caribbean (ECLAC) (2007) 'Women's contribution to equality in Latin America and the Caribbean', 10th Session of the Regional Conference on Women in Latin America and the Caribbean, Quito, 6–9 August.

FAO (2001) *Targeting for Nutrition Improvement: Resources for Advancing Nutritional Wellbeing*, Food and Agriculture Organization of the United Nations, Rome, Italy.

Folbre, N. (2006) 'Measuring care: gender, empowerment, and the care economy', *Journal of Human Development and Capabilities* 7:2, pp. 183–199.

Folbre, N. (2009) 'Valuing unpaid work matters, especially for the poor', *The New York Times*, 21 September, http://economix.blogs.nytimes.com/2009/09/21/valuing-unpaid-work-matters-especially-for-the-poor/ (last accessed 14 May 2010).

Friedman, J. and Thomas, D. (2007) 'Psychological health before, during, and after an economic crisis: results from Indonesia, 1993–2000', *The World Bank Economic Review*, Policy Research Working Paper Series 4386.

Hanushek, E. and Wobmann, L. (2007) 'The role of education quality in economic growth', World Bank Policy Research Working Paper No. 4122, World Bank, Washington, DC.

Harper, C. and Jones, N. (2010) 'Turning crisis into opportunity for children affected by HIV/AIDS', ODI Background Note, ODI, London.

Harper, C., Jones, N. and McKay, A., 'Including children in policy responses to economic crises: lessons from the past and policies for a sustainable future', UNICEF Working Paper, UNICEF, New York.

Heckman, J.J. (2008) 'Schools, skills, and synapses', *Economic Inquiry* 46:3, pp. 289–324.

Heckman, J.J. and Masterov, D.V. (2007) 'The productivity argument for investing in young children', Working Paper 13016, National Bureau of Economic Research, Cambridge, UK.

Heymann, J. (2006) *Forgotton Families: Ending the Growing Crisis Confronting Children and Working Parents in the Global Economy*, Oxford: Oxford University Press.

Holmes, R. and Jones, N. (2009a) 'Gender inequality, risk and vulnerability in the rural economy: re-focusing the public works agenda to take account of economic and social risks', background report for SOFA 2010, ODI, London.

Holmes, R. and Jones, N. (2009b) 'Putting the social back into social protection', ODI Background Note, ODI, London.

Holmes, R., Jones, N. and Marsden, H. (2009) 'Gender vulnerabilities, food price shocks and social protection responses', ODI Background Note, ODI, London.

Hossain, N. Eyben, R. et al. (2009) *Accounts of Crisis: Poor People's Experiences of the Food, Fuel and Financial Crises in Five Countries*, IDS, Brighton, Sussex.

ILO (2009) *The Financial and Economic Crisis: A Decent Work Response*, ILO, Geneva, Switzerland.

Jones, N. (2009) 'Promoting synergies between child protection and social protection', Briefing Paper: Social Policies, UNICEF and ODI, Dakar and London.

Jones, N. and Marsden, H. (2009) 'Assessing the impacts of and policy responses to the 1997–1998 Asian financial crisis through a child rights lens', report commissioned by UNICEF, ODI, London.

Kabeer, N. (2008) *Mainstreaming Gender in Social Protection for the Informal Economy*, Commonwealth Secretariat, London.

Kahn, R.S., Brandt, D. and Whitaker, R.C. (2004) 'Combined effect of mothers' and fathers' mental health symptoms on children's behavioural and emotional well-being', *Archives of Pediatric and Adolescent Medicine* 158, pp. 721–729.

Kain, J. (2002) 'Chile's school feeding programme: targeting experience', *Nutrition Research* 22:5, pp. 599–608.

Kizilirmak, B. and Memis, E. (2009) 'The unequal burden of poverty on time use', Levy Economics Institute Working Paper no. 572, The Levy Economics Institute, Bard College, New York.

Klijn, F. (1998) 'Aral, an island in time: continuities and change in a Kyrghyz mountain community', MA dissertation, University of Amsterdam.

Knowles, J.C., Ernesto, M.P. and Racelis, M. (1999) 'Social consequences of the financial crisis in Asia', Economic Staff Paper no. 60, Asian Development Bank, Manila, Philippines.

Kuehnast, K. and Dudwick, N. (2002) 'Better a hundred friends than a hundred rubles? Social networks in transition – the Kyrgyz Republic', *World Bank Economists Forum* 2, pp. 51–88.

Lotrakul, M. (2006) 'Suicide in Thailand during the period 1998–2003', *Psychiatry and Clinical Neurosciences* 60, pp. 90–95.

Lund, F. (2002) 'Consensus and contestation: the policy for child support in South Africa', draft monograph, School of Development Studies, University of Natal.

Lund, F. (2009) 'The provision of care by non-household institutions', Research Report 3, School of Development Studies, University of KwaZulu-Natal, Durban, South Africa.

MacDonald, M., Phipps, S. and Lethbridge, L. (2005) 'Taking its toll: the influence of paid and unpaid work on women's well-being', *Feminist Economics* 11:1, pp. 63–94.

McCord, A. and Vandermootele, M. (2009) 'The global financial crisis: poverty and social protection: evidence from 10 country case studies', Briefing Paper no. 51, ODI, London.

Marcus, R. (2009) 'Transition to a market economy and children's rights: Kyrgyzstan in regional perspective', background paper commissioned by UNICEF, ODI, New York, London.

Pereznieto, P. (forthcoming) 'The impact of economic shocks on children in Latin America: the case of Mexico's 1995 Peso crisis and Argentina's 2002 convertibility crisis', background paper commissioned by UNICEF, ODI, New York, London.

Pereznieto, P. and Jones, N. (2005) 'The social impact of trade liberalization: how can childhood poverty be reduced?', Young Lives Policy Brief no. 1, Save the Children, London.

Putnam, R. (2004) 'Education, diversity, social cohesion and "social capital"', note for discussion presented at the meeting of OECD education ministers: Raising the Quality of Learning for All, Dublin, Ireland.

Quisumbing, A., Meinzen-Dick, R. and Bassett, L. (2008) 'Helping women respond to the global food price crisis', Policy Brief 7, IFRPI, Washington, DC.

Razavi, S. (2007) 'The political and social economy of care in a development context: conceptual issues, research questions and policy options', Political and Social Economy of Care Series, Paper no. 3, Gender and Development Research Programme, UNRISD, Geneva, Switzerland.

Ruiz-Casares, M. and Heymann, J. (2009) *Children Home Alone Unsupervised: Modeling Parental Decisions and Associated Factors in Botswana*, IHSP, Mexico, Vietnam, Montreal.

Sánchez, M.V. and Vos, R. (2009) 'Impact of the global crisis on the achievement of the MDGs in Latin America', DESA Working Paper no. 74, United Nations Department of Economic and Social Affairs, New York.

Sirimanne, S. (2009) 'The gender perspectives of the financial crisis', Commission on the Status of Women Fifty-third Session, New York, 2–13 March 2009.

Suharto, E. (2007) 'Social protection for children in difficult situations. Lessons from Indonesia and ASEAN', paper presented at the International Seminar on Asian Families in Transition, Challenges for Social Work Intervention, Indonesia.

The London Summit (2009) 'Global plan for recovery and reform', official communique issued at the close of the G20 London Summit, www.londonsummit.gov.uk/resources/en/PDF/final-communique (last accessed 8 January 2010).

Truong, T.A. (2000) 'A feminist perspective on the Asian miracle and crisis: enlarging the conceptual map of human development', *Journal of Human Development* 1:1, pp. 159–164.

UNDP (2009) *The Second Periodic Progress Report on the Millennium Development Goals in the Kyrgyz Republic*, UNDP, Bishkek, Kyrgyzstan.

UNIFEM (2009) 'Making economic stimulus packages work for women and gender equality', UNIFEM Working Paper, UNIFEM, New York.

World Bank (2009) 'Conditional cash transfers: reducing present and future poverty', World Bank Policy Research Report, The World Bank, Washington, DC.

About the authors

Jessica Espey is an Economic Policy Advisor within the Development Policy Team at Save the Children, in London.

Caroline Harper is Head of Programme and a research fellow at the ODI in London, is leader of the Social Development Programme, and is Associate Director of the Chronic Poverty Research Centre.

Nicola Jones is Programme Leader and research fellow within the Social Development Programme at ODI in London.

Resources

Liz Cooke

'Gender perspectives on the global economic crisis' (2010), Richard King and Caroline Sweetman, Oxfam International Discussion Paper, www.oxfam.org. uk/resources/policy/economic_crisis/gender-perspectives-economic-crisis. html, 18 pp.

This paper summarizes the issues raised during a workshop of development and gender practitioners and academics, convened in September 2009, by *Gender & Development*. How the effects of the economic crisis are experienced depends, to a large extent, on women's and men's relationships with the people and institutions with whom they interact. These relationships are profoundly different for women and men. Unemployment hits poor families hard, regardless of whether it is a man or woman who is laid off. However, the chances of a family recovering from this setback is shaped by the different levels of bargaining power that women and men have in the labour market, and their different responsibilities at home. The gender inequalities and power imbalances that predate the current crisis have resulted in its additional afflictions falling disproportionately on those who are already structurally disempowered and marginalized. Although often labelled 'coping strategies', the means women find to respond to crises are frequently unsustainable, and are more appropriately conceived of as 'desperation measures'. Pre-existing inequalities, which include under-representation of women at all levels of economic decision-making and their over-representation in informal, vulnerable, and casual employment, are often more significant than gender inequalities arising specifically from the crisis. The paper includes sections on 'Conceptualizing the crisis', 'Assessing the crisis', and 'Pro-poor, gender-sensitive policy responses'.

'The current economic and financial crisis: a gender perspective' (2009), Rania Antonopoulos, Working Paper No. 562, The Levy Economics Institute of Bard College, www.levy.org/vdoc.aspx?docid=1145, 43 pp.

In this paper, Rania Antonopoulos, after outlining the current crisis and the need for a gender perspective to be central to any analysis and response, explores the recent (as of spring 2009) and likely effects of the crisis in various sectors – what she terms the 'visible and invisible gendered paths of transmission [of the crisis] in the world of work'. She provides an extremely useful discussion of the crisis and gender in relation to: paid work in the export sectors of textiles, agriculture, and tourism; informal work and vulnerable workers;

unpaid work and 'invisible' vulnerabilities; remittances; and food security. She then moves on to discuss what gendered policy responses would look like in the areas of: the financial sector – for example, the protection of microcredit lending to women and the importance of gender-aware fiscal stimulation policies (such as state-sponsored job creation schemes targeting women, including some successful examples of this); food and nutrition (where access to land rights, extension services, and production links to the mainstream economy are vital for women); and aid flows (highlighting the importance to women in developing countries of the honouring by donor countries of their overseas development aid commitments in health and education).

Taking Stock: The Financial Crisis and Development from a Feminist Perspective (January 2010), Ursula Dullnig, Brita Neuhold, Traude Novy, Kathrin Pelzer, Edith Schnitzer, Barbara Schöllenberger, and Claudia Thallmayer, WIDE's position paper on the global social, economic and environmental crisis, http://62.149.193.10/wide/download/TakingStock_WIDEaustriaEN.pdf?id= 1110, 41 pp.
In this paper, Women in Development Europe (WIDE) presents a feminist analysis of the global economic crisis, making the point that there are fundamental connections between the financial crisis and both the care crisis and the environmental/climate change crisis. The paper's essential premise is that – in a context in which 'the small window of opportunity that the crisis opened for fundamental [financial] reform seems to be closing again' – a much broader view of economics needs to be adopted, one in which the free play of market forces, cut loose from any social and ecological considerations is abandoned, and the paradigm of unlimited growth is replaced by one in which the economy is defined as 'the sphere of social activities which are related to the provision of the goods and services which can maintain life and support its output'. The paper outlines the background to the current crisis – the end of fixed exchange rates, deregulation of financial markets, globalization, and the 'detonator' of the crisis, sub-prime mortgages in the US – the bailing out of the banks, and who is paying for the crisis, the gender-specific outcomes of the interrelated crises, and the effects on funding for international development. The final section of the paper provides a checklist of proposals for ways forward for national governments and the EU, headed by the steps necessary for bringing about a 'radical change of mentality'.

'The world economic and financial crisis: what will it mean for gender equality?' (2009), speech given by Ines Alberdi, Executive Director, UNIFEM, www. unifem.org/news_events/story_detail.php?StoryID=901, 6 pp.
This speech by the Executive Director of UNIFEM – the United Nations Development Fund for Women – focuses on the gendered impact of the crisis on employment, and provides a useful overview of the subject. For Ms Alberdi, with up to 22 million women possibly losing their jobs, gender equality gains

both at home and at work are being jeopardized. Her speech includes examples of gendered job losses in the export processing sector in Asia/Pacific, Africa, and Central America and touches on the informal economy; migrant labour; the increased risk of gender-based violence; and girl child mortality. She goes on to discuss the need for a gendered analysis of crisis response packages, the importance of sex-disaggregated data collection and reporting, and the importance of overseas development aid. In conclusion, Ms Alberdi outlines some opportunities presented by the crisis; not least, the chance for policymakers to rethink the fundamental economic assumption of the 'male breadwinner'. These include a growth in the 'green economy', with an opportunity for countries to provide training and information to women to enable them to compete on a level playing field, and the invention of a new kind of 'green revolution', this time focusing on women small farmers, who constitute the majority of food-staple producers, in order to break out of dependency on international commodity markets and food imports.

Emerging Issue: The Gender Perspectives of the Financial Crisis (2009), Commission on the Status of Women, UN Division for the Advancement of Women, www.un.org/womenwatch/daw/csw/53sess.htm#themes
Through a series of different documents, this website reports on a panel at the Commission on the Status of Women, 2009, on the gender perspectives of the global economic crisis. Some of the points made were: economic recessions put a disproportionate burden on women, who are more likely to be made redundant than men (as men are traditionally considered to be the main 'breadwinners'), and have unequal access to and control over economic and financial resources; increasing unemployment and decreasing household incomes means that women and girls often need to take on unpaid work, including caregiving. Women may also be forced into informal employment, where they have few rights and restricted social protection and benefits; cuts in public spending in the light of economic crises, for example in the areas of health and education, can reduce women's and girls' access to basic services; girls may be withdrawn from schools to help with household work during times of economic crisis, reinforcing gender gaps in education.

The panel's recommendations included: governments, international organizations and civil society, including the private sector, should play an active role in ensuring that financial and economic crises do not have a disproportionate negative impact on women and girls; policy responses to financial crises should be people-centred and focus on employment, sustainability and gender equality, and they should aim to enhance productivity, in particular in agriculture, a critical sector for women in developing countries; women's entrepreneurial capacity should be strengthened; gender-responsive budgeting should be conducted as a strategy for responding to the different priorities and needs of women and men; and public funds should be invested in care services that reduce women's unpaid domestic and care work and design policies that promote equal sharing of responsibilities between men and women. The website hosts an issues paper, a report of the panel meeting (in English, French, Spanish, Arabic, Chinese and Russian), and the papers presented by the panellists.

The Global Financial Crisis: Assessing Vulnerability for Women and Children (2009), Shwetlena Sabarwal, Nistha Sinha and Mayra Buvinic, The World Bank, www.world bank.org/financialcrisis/pdf/Women-Children-Vulnerability-March09.pdf, 4 pp.
Arguing that the current global economic crisis (on top of recent food price increases) will have serious, gender-specific consequences for women and children in poor countries, the authors of this concise paper set out seven 'main messages' regarding gender and the crisis, which include discussion of: the 'added worker' effect, which sees more women entering the workforce, taking up jobs in an attempt to boost family income (something witnessed during the Latin American crisis of the mid-1990s and the East Asian crisis at the end of the same decade); the fact that girls in poor countries with pre-existing low female schooling rates are highly vulnerable to being pulled out of school as households cope with declining income; and the loss of women's income having long-term negative implications for the welfare of poor households (which may be greater than a similar loss in men's income) because of both the contributions women make to current household income, and their 'preference' for investing scare resources on child well-being. The final 'message' outlines the 2009 response to the crisis of The World Bank Group Gender Action Plan.

Global Employment Trends for Women (2009), International Labour Organization, www.ilo.org/global/What_we_do/Publications/lang--en/docName--WCMS_103456/index.htm, 78 pp.
This issue of the *Global Employment Trends for Women* series looks at the gender aspects of the impact of the financial crisis and slowdown in world economic growth on jobs, and updates indicators on the situation of women in labour markets around the world.

'Paying the price for the economic crisis' (2009), Bethan Emmett, Oxfam International Discussion Paper, www.oxfam.org.uk/resources/policy/economic_crisis/downloads/impact_economic_crisis_women.pdf, 15 pp.
This paper presents the findings of research undertaken by Oxfam International in February 2009, in which women working in global supply chains in 10 countries across Asia and Latin America were interviewed about how the economic crisis was affecting their lives and families. The research suggests that global markets are pushing the costs of the crisis onto women and children in developing countries. As supply chains are squeezed by falling global demand, women in export manufacturing are often the first to be laid off, with employers leaving pay outstanding and evading legal obligations to give notice and

pay compensation, and governments turning a blind eye. The lives of women who were already vulnerable and exploited have become even more precarious.

'Tracking the impact of the global economic crisis – ten things women's groups can investigate' (2010), Diane Elson, *Gender & Development* 18(1): 143–5, available at www.genderanddevelopment.org
Highlighting the lack of information available on the human impact of the crisis and its gendered effects, in this short piece feminist economist Diane Elson suggests 10 areas which researchers could focus their attention on, such as jobs in wage or salary employment, cutbacks in public expenditure, and migrants' remittances, setting out questions designed to elicit from respondents the sort of data currently lacking from many analyses of the crisis.

Impact of the Crisis on Women's Rights: Sub Regional Perspectives (2009), Association for Women's Rights in Development Brief Series, www.awid.org/eng/About-AWID/AWID-News/Brief-Series-Impact-of-the-crisis-on-women-sub-regional-perspectives
In this extremely helpful set of briefings commissioned by the Association for Women's Rights in Development (AWID), the authors report on the impact of the crisis in eight different regions: Latin America, the Caribbean, Asia, the Pacific Islands, Central Asia, Western Africa, Western Europe, and Eastern Europe, with briefings coming soon from Eastern, Southern and Central Africa, the Middle East and North Africa, the USA, plus a cross-regional analysis. In their briefings, the authors explore answers to a number of questions posed by AWID, including: whether there have been any identifiable concrete actions or initiatives in response to the crisis which have either negatively or positively affected women's lives, and what the potential future impacts of a global recession are on women in each region.

Women's Poverty and Social Exclusion in the European Union at a time of Recession: An Invisible Crisis? (2010), Oxfam International/European Women's Lobby, www.oxfam.org.uk/resources/policy/economic_crisis/economic-crisis-women-poverty-exclusion-eu.html, 38 pp.
All over the world, women remain poor in relation to men. This also is true in every member state of the European Union (EU). The persistence of poverty in such a rich region of the world is shocking, even before the impact of recession has been considered. In October 2009, Oxfam and the European Women's Lobby, commissioned research to explore and analyse the hidden impact of the current economic recession on women's poverty in the EU, and this subsequent report documents evidence from across the continent of: precarious working conditions; increasing discrimination in the labour market with a subsequent shift to informal work; rising levels of poverty; reduced access to services; and rising levels of domestic violence, accompanied by cuts in vital support services.

The evidence clearly indicates that the recession is already having a significant negative effect on the lives of women, not only in relation to the labour market, but also, crucially, outside it. However, the impact of the recession on women remains largely invisible and further in-depth analysis is urgently required. The paper ends with a set of policy recommendations.

'Women paying the price: the impact of the global financial crisis on women in Southeast Asia' (2010), Yada Praparpun, Oxfam GB research report, www. oxfam.org.uk/resources/policy/economic_crisis/economic-crisis-impact-on-southeast-asia.html, 51 pp.
Drawing on evidence from country case studies from Thailand, Philippines, Cambodia, Vietnam, and Indonesia, this report seeks to identify how the financial crisis has affected women, in order test whether Southeast Asian governments are doing enough to support the most vulnerable. The individual country reports found that the female employment situation in the export manufacturing and service sectors, for example, textiles, electronics, and tourism has been seriously affected, with large numbers of women either losing their jobs, or being forced to accept reduced working hours for less income. Remittances from migrants, either internal or external, have also been negatively affected, with many women who migrated to the cities for work, rather than serving as financial support for their families in the countryside, now becoming dependent on their rural families for support. The report concludes with recommended short- and long-term policy responses.

'Rural women earning income in Indonesian factories: the impact on gender relations' (2001), Peter Hancock, *Gender & Development* 9(1): 18–24, www. genderanddevelopment.org
In 1997 and 1998, the international economic crisis widely known as the 'Asian crisis' caused massive inflation and currency devaluation in Indonesia. This paper highlights the effects of the economic crisis on rural Indonesian women and their families. After the crisis, young women who were employed in factories began to contribute a significantly greater amount of their wages to family budgets. This cash contribution seems not only to have altered the nature of household livelihood strategies, but also to have raised young women's status within the household.

'In times of crisis, women can be agents of change' (2009), interview with Otaviano Canuto, Vice President and Head of the Poverty Reduction and Economic Management Network, The World Bank, in *Gender Equality as Smart Economics*, World Bank, http://siteresources.worldbank.org/INTGENDER/Resources/336003-1205954955184/OtavianoCauto.pdf, 2 pp.
In this short interview, Otaviano Canuto discusses the vulnerability of women and girls in developing countries in economic crises – particularly in countries, mostly in Africa, that are affected by both low female schooling and high

infant and child deaths – arguing that many more girls than boys die when there are negative economic shocks, and not jus t in regions that have historically demonstrated a 'boy preference'. Maternal health is also put at risk, as is women's income, as a result of employment losses in export-oriented industries, tightening micro-finance lending, and slowing remittances. Mr Canuto, however, stresses that although women and girls are vulnerable to the crisis, The World Bank believes that if they are given the opportunity, they can be powerful agents of change. With women usually reinvesting a much higher part of their earnings in their families and communities than men, they spread wealth and create a positive impact on future development. Crisis response programmes, which he outlines, must be made to work for women – 'it is good economics to do so'.

Lessons not Learned? Gender, Employment and Social Protection in Asia's Crisis-affected Export Sectors (2009), Samantha Hung, Asian Development Bank, www.adb.org/Documents/Events/2009/Poverty-Social-Development/P3-gender-impact-crisis-Hung-paper.pdf, 24 pp.
This clearly written paper argues that more than 10 years on from the Asian economic crisis, in the Asian export sector, women continue to be a part of the similarly gender-segregated and gender-inequitable industry patterns which saw them disproportionately affected in 1997–98. For the author, a failure to respond to the gendered effects of a decline in the Asian export industry means setting back gender equality gains, and rising poverty for huge numbers of women and their families. The paper presents the results of six country field studies which investigated the impacts of the current crisis on selected export industries, providing evidence of the effects the crisis is having, and outlines the kind of gendered policy responses which should be implemented. These would include economic stimulus packages aimed at the particular export sectors in which women workers predominate, rather than as traditionally, sectors such as construction and physical infrastructure; the rebalancing of labour markets, redesigning education and training so as to expand occupational choices for women and to redress male breadwinner bias; 'pro-women' infrastructure investment by governments, such as clinics and hospitals; the strengthening of gender-responsive social protection and social services; and gender mainstreaming in any economic stimulus, including monitoring and evaluation.

Gender and Social Protection in Asia: What does the Crisis Change? (2009), Nicola Jones and Rebecca Holmes, Overseas Development Institute, www.adb.org/documents/events/2009/Poverty-Social-Development/P3-gender-social-protection-ODI-paper.pdf, 32 pp.
This paper examines social protection responses to the current global economic crisis and seeks to assess the extent to which they are responding adequately to the gendered experiences of poverty and vulnerability in four country case studies – Bangladesh, India, Indonesia, and Viet Nam. The authors draw

on an extensive desk review and preliminary fieldwork findings from the larger Gender and Social Protection Effectiveness project funded by the UK Department for International Development and the Australian Agency for International Development, in order to highlight areas in which gender-responsive social protection policy and programme interventions could be strengthened, both to cushion women, men, and children from the worst effects of the crisis in the short term, and also to develop a stronger social policy infrastructure to support poor and vulnerable citizens more effectively in the case of future global economic crises.

The Possible Impact of the Global Slowdown on Maternal, Newborn and Child Health in Asia (2009), Ian Anderson and Basil Rodriques, www.adb.org/documents/events/2009/Poverty-Social-Development/impact-on-mother-and-child-health-Anderson-Rodriques-paper.pdf, 14 pp.
For the authors of this paper, the current economic crisis presents both risks and opportunities. They argue that despite Asia having been the fastest growing region in the world for decades, the region accounted for nearly 34 per cent of global deaths of children under five, more than 40 per cent of maternal deaths, and 60 per cent of newborn deaths worldwide. For the authors, the level and pattern of health expenditure in Asia helps, in part, to explain not just these poor health outcomes for women and children, but levels of poverty and inequity as well; nutrition and health care costs for families can quickly become 'catastrophic', driving households below the poverty line and threatening their long-term health. The risk is that the economic crisis will only serve to exacerbate these existing problems. However, the authors also believe that the current crisis offers opportunities, and a spur, to improve the effectiveness, efficiency, and equity of health expenditure. Tight budgets and fiscal stringency means governments have even greater need to make health budgets more efficient, effective, and equitable. They suggest that an initiative such as well-targeted conditional cash transfers can, simultaneously, improve health and nutrition outcomes; protect the poor from impoverishment; and be a counter-cyclical stimulus to the economy. They caution, however, that broader, health-strengthening reforms are also needed.

'Leading by example – protecting the most vulnerable during the economic crisis' (2009), The Global Campaign for the Health Millennium Development Goals, www.ausaid.gov.au/publications/pdf/lead_by_example.pdf, 59 pp.
This progress report published by the Global Campaign for the Health Millennium Development Goals (MDGs), on behalf of the Network of Global Leaders, focuses on MDGs 4 and 5, which relate specifically to child and maternal health. Based on the lessons of previous economic crises, the report recommends urgent measures to get MDGs 4 and 5 'back on track', so as to meet the 2015 targets, despite the current crisis. Country members of the Network, and other key stakeholders, for example, United Nations agencies and

civil society organizations, set out the specific actions they are taking to ensure the MDGs are met and the effects of the global economic crisis are mitigated, and outline the 'Maternal, Newborn, and Child Health Consensus', a plan of action which the authors believe is all the more crucial to adhere to given the threat posed by the global economic crisis.

'Recovering from economic and financial crisis: food security and safety nets' (2010), Joint Meeting of the Executive boards of UNDP/UNFPA, UNICEF and WFP, UNDP, UNFPA, UNICEF, and WFP, www.unicef.org/about/execboard/files/B-9371E-JMB_10_WFP_coordinated_paper_-_12_Jan_10_version.pdf, 9 pp. Arguing that hunger and food insecurity retard growth and development, this short paper, with a focus on food security and safety nets and related social protection interventions, outlines national and international efforts to address and recover from the impacts of the economic crisis. Examples of how the United Nations Development Programme, United Nations Population Fund, United Nations Children's Fund, and World Food Programme are working to support and strengthen these efforts are provided, and priorities for promoting food security and reducing vulnerability during the recovery are discussed, with their implications for the four United Nations agencies outlined. The paper mentions 'the poor', 'poor consumers' and 'households', and 'families', but does not discuss any gender differences which may operate within these categories, although it recognizes that 'girls are more likely affected than boys' with regard to a possible increase in already high infant mortality rates, and that the impact of 'increased violence, especially against girls and women, sexual trafficking, and other negative outcomes', caused by a prolonged period of high domestic food prices, could be significant.

'Reclaiming institutional and policy space amidst crisis' (2009), Marina Durano, Gigi Francisco and Gita Sen, *Development* 52(3): 334–7, www.dawnnet.org/uploads/documents/PAPER_Amidst%20Crisis_Durano,%20Francisco,%20Sen_2009_DEV%20TS7%2052_PEG.pdf, 4 pp.
In this paper, the authors, representing Development Alternatives with Women for a New Era, argue that with regard to the economic crisis, the critical question now is not only policies to overcome it, but also which global institutions should play what roles. They argue that in this time of unprecedented crisis, the United Nations (UN), in order to play a renewed and vigorous role needs women as much as women have historically needed the UN.

'Promoting gender equality through stimulus packages and public job creation: lessons learned from South Africa's Expanded Public Works Programme' (2009), Public policy brief No. 101, Rania Antonopoulos, The Levy Economics Institute of Bard College, www.levyinstitute.org/publications/?docid=1154, 12 pp.
Joblessness – increased levels of which are a feature of the economic crisis – is associated with greater levels of poverty, marginalization, and social exclusion.

In this paper, the author proposes an extension to the existing Expanded Public Works Programme (EPWP) in South Africa – a job creation initiative introduced in 2004 – which would see a new sector for social service delivery in health and education being created. With current EPWP projects focused on labour-intensive infrastructure, the author argues that jobs created in the areas of early childhood development and community-based care would not only meet policy objectives of income and job generation, the provisioning of communities' unmet needs, skill enhancement for a new group of workers, but also promote gender equality by addressing the overtaxed time of women, who are predominantly those who undertake unpaid caring work for children and the sick. A four-page summary of the paper is also available at www.levy-institute.org/pubs/hili_101a.pdf

Vision for a Better World: From Economic Crisis to Equality (2010), Devaki Jain and Diane Elson, in collaboration with the Casablanca Dreamers, United Nations Development Programme, www.casablanca-dream.net/literature/index.html, 31 pp.
This well-considered and well-written paper manages to cover a lot of ground, without overwhelming the reader. Challenging the idea that the desirable outcome of policy responses to the current set of crises is a return to 'normal', and drawing on the feminist political economy conception of economic activity as a system of provisioning, guided by social norms, and structured by social interests, the authors argue for alternatives that not only offer an effective response, but which facilitate a transition towards the creation of more just and inclusive economies. The paper is divided into four sections.

Section One focuses on the gender dimensions of the recent and ongoing crises of not only finance and employment, but also deprivation of food, water, energy, fuel, and care; and of environmental devastation. Section Two presents illustrations of the uneven progress in implementing the Beijing Platform for Action (BpfA), noting that much recent 'progress' is built on forms of development that are environmentally and socially unsustainable, and generate inequality. Section Three discusses the challenges and opportunities facing feminism and women's movements in their struggle for a better, more equal world, and Section Four sets out some ideas on economic policies that would support a more equal, just, peaceful, and democratic world, in which the BPfA is fully realized for all women and men.

Bringing Human Rights to Bear in Times of Crisis: A Human Rights Analysis of Government Responses to the Economic Crisis (2010), Aldo Caliari, Sally-Anne Way, Natalie Raaber, Anne Schoenstein, Radhika Baladrishnan, and Nicolas Lusiani, AWID, Center of Concern, Center for Economic and Social Rights, Centre for Women's Global Leadership, ESCR-Net, www.escr-net.org/usr_doc/HRResponsestoEconCrisis_Final.pdf, 24 pp.

Prepared for the thirteenth Session of the United Nations (UN) Human Rights Council and its High Level Segment on the impact of the global economic and financial crises to the realization of all human rights, this paper seeks to analyse government responses to the crisis from a human rights perspective, examining how governments' actions worldwide have lived up to or let down their human rights obligations. Arguing that states, as primary duty-bearers of human rights obligations, must use the maximum of available resources to create the conditions under which all people living under their jurisdiction can exercise their full range of economic and social rights, the authors examine governments' responses, such as stimulus packages, social protection, and support to the financial sector through a human rights lens, and look at how trade, debt, and aid act as international constraints to effecting a human rights response. The paper concludes with a set of recommendations for national governments, the international community, and the UN Human Rights Council

'Unlocking the development box: markers along the way towards a gender sensitive development agenda' (2009), Mariama Williams, a preliminary issue paper, International Gender and Trade Network, www.web.igtn.org/home/index.php?option=com_docman&task=cat_view&gid=118&ItemId=6, 77 pp. In this thoughtful paper, the author discusses issues, especially as they relate to trade and finance, which are of critical importance to economic development in the global South, within the current context of the global economic crisis, the food crisis, the HIV/AIDS pandemic, the global war on terror, and climate change. The first part of the paper includes a discussion on globalization and the economic crisis, a critique of the neoliberal approach to development, and heterodox and feminist views on the macroeconomics of development, and goes on to examine the question of economic development in the global South; what is it, who is it for, and how best to secure it; and the final section looks at the debates around alternatives. The appendices provide some helpful explanations and definitions of some of the economic terminology and ideas included in the main body of the paper.

'Gender biases in finance' (2001), Irene van Staveren, *Gender & Development* 9(1): 9–17, www.genderanddevelopment.org
This paper discusses some of the relationships between gender relations and finance, particularly at the meso- and macro-levels of financial transactions and trends. The author focuses on gender-based inequalities in finance, and the gender-based inefficiencies in finance that are created as a result, arguing that these gender biases in finance perpetuate both inequalities between women and men, and poverty.

'Let women tame the macho excess' (1 December 2008), *Management Today*, www.managementtoday.co.uk/search/article/865053/let-women-tame-macho-excess/

Amidst the huge amount of coverage devoted to the causes of the financial and economic crisis in the media in the North, were suggestions that the crisis was literally 'man'-made, and that had more women been employed in the traditionally competitive, risk-taking, macho finance sector, the crisis might have been averted. This piece provides an interesting example of the discussions in the media on this issue, centring on the appointment of two women to run newly nationalized banks in Iceland, as the country sought to recover from its financial meltdown.

Meltdown: The End of the Age of Greed (2009), Paul Mason, Verso, website: www. versobooks.com, ISBN: 978-1844673964, 198 pp.

Fool's Gold: How Unrestrained Greed Corrupted A Dream, Shattered Global Markets And Unleashed a Catastrophe (2009), Gillian Tett, Little, Brown, website: www. littlebrown.co.uk/home, ISBN: 978-1408701676, 301 pp.

Chasing Alpha: How Reckless Growth and Unchecked Ambition Ruined the City's Golden Decade (2009), Philip Augar, Bodley Head, website: www.bodley head.co.uk, ISBN 978-1847920362, 272 pp.

For readers interested in understanding how the worst global economic downturn since the Depression of the 1930s was brought about, these three titles describe, from a UK/US perspective, how financial practices in the North precipitated a global crisis. In *Meltdown*, BBC journalist Paul Mason describes the destruction of Northern investment banks that brought the global economy to the brink of collapse, and examines the consequences, which may include a much more tightly regulated financial sector. Gillian Tett, Assistant Editor of the *Financial Times*, in her book, *Fool's Gold*, looks at the crisis through the experience of the investment bank J.P. Morgan, where many of the complex derivatives that helped bring down the system, were developed. In *Chasing Alpha*, Philip Augar charts the 10 years in which the UK 'tried to reinvent itself as a hedge fund crossed with an offshore tax haven', only to see the failure of one bank after another in 2007, with the government taking controlling stakes in the banking sector, and the reputation of the City in ruins.

Organizations

Association for Women's Rights in Development (AWID), 215 Spadina Ave, Suite 150, Toronto, Ontario, M5T 2C7, Canada, tel: +1 416 594 3773, email: contact@awid.org, website: www.awid.org/eng/About-AWID/AWID-Initiatives/ IDeA/Systemic-Crisis

The AWID website's section, 'The global crisis: feminist analysis and information', features a wide range of information on gender and the economic crisis, with news, analysis, and interviews on the impact of the crisis, information on how global institutions, civil society organizations, and women's rights organizations and movements are responding, along with a section on taking action, featuring opportunities for participation, events listings, and links to other organizations working on the crisis.

Development Alternatives with Women for a New Era (DAWN), c/o Women and Gender Institute, Miriam College, Katipunan Road, Loyola Heights, QC 1108, NCR, Philippines, tel: +63 2 434 6440, email: info@dawnnet. org, website: www.dawnnet.org/research-analyses.php?theme_1

DAWN has long been engaged in research and analysis on economics and gender, and its work on the current economic crisis can be found in its 'Research and analyses' section, on the 'Political economy of globalization' pages.

Institute for Development Studies (IDS), University of Sussex, IDS at the University of Sussex, Brighton, BN1 9RE, tel: +44 (0)1273 606261, email: ids@ids.ac.uk, website: www.ids.ac.uk/go/research-teams/vulnerability-and-poverty-reduction-team/centrefor-social-protection/crisis-watch

The 'Crisis watch' pages on the IDS website bring together IDS research on the impact of the crisis, including crisis research tools, and information on projects exploring the impact of past and present crises. There are also links to other organizations working on the crisis, and a list of publications on the crisis, to which visitors to the site can suggest additions.

International Labour Organization (ILO), 4 route des Morillons, CH-1211 Geneva 22, Switzerland, tel: +41 (0) 22 799 6111, email: ilo@ilo.org, website: www.ilo.org/pls/apex/f?p=109:3:4005908237074235::NO::P3_SUBJECT:GENDER

The ILO's 'Global Jobs Crisis Observatory' pages on their website feature a gender section, which provides ILO 'tools and good practices' relating to gender, and relevant to discussions on the economic crisis and recovery, and also resources on gender and the crisis from a variety of sources, presented under the headings: gender dimension, employment, and migration.

Oxfam GB, Oxfam House, John Smith Drive, Oxford, OX4 2JY, UK, tel: +44 (0)1865 473727, website: www.oxfam.org.uk/economiccrisis

The issue of gender has been central to Oxfam's research on the economic crisis. On the economic crisis section of Oxfam GB's website can be found links to all the organization's research reports on the crisis, including those with a specific focus on gender, plus statistics on the crisis, and an outline of Oxfam's response.

United Nations Development Fund for Women (UNIFEM), 304 East 45th Street 15th Floor, New York, NY 10017, USA, tel: +1 212 906-6400, email: via website, website: www.unifem.org

While the UNIFEM website has no specific section dedicated to the economic crisis, UNIFEM resources on and activities around the crisis can be found on the site, and a search brings up a comprehensive list of relevant content.

UN Non Governmental Liaison Service (UN- NGLS), Geneva Office: Palais des Nations, 1211 Geneva 10, Switzerland, tel. +41 22 917 2076, email: ngls@ unctad.org, New York Office: Room DC1-1106, United Nations, New York NY 10017, USA, tel: +1 212 963 3125, email: ngls@un.org, website: www.un-ngls. org/spip.php?page=infocus&id_mot=8

The UN-NGLS was created in 1975 by several agencies of the UN system to serve as a bridge between the UN and civil society organizations. Its website provides information on UN/CSO engagement and resources on various issues, including the economic crisis.

Women in Informal Employment: Globalizing and Organizing (WIEGO), website:www.wiego.org

WIEGO is a global research policy network that seeks to improve the status of the working poor, especially women, in the informal economy. Its website publishes research and resources on the subject, including the economic crisis.

WomenWatch, Inter-Agency Network on Women and Gender Equality, 2 United Nations Plaza, 12th floor, New York, NY 10017, USA, email: womenwatch@ un.org, website: www.un.org/womenwatch/feature/financialcrisis

The United Nations (UN)'s interagency WomenWatch website brings together information and resources on gender equality issues from across the UN. Its section, 'The gender perspectives of the financial crisis', provides access to relevant content from UN agencies, including: UN Development Fund for Women (UNIFEM), UN Economic and Social Commission for Asia and the Pacific (UNESCAP), UN Educational, Scientific and Cultural Organization (UNESCO), and UN International Research and Training Institute for the Advancement of Women (UN-INSTRAW).

The World Bank, Gender and Development Group, Poverty Reduction and Economic Management, World Bank, 1818 H Street, Washington DC 20433, USA, tel: +1 202 473 0205, email: pic@worldbank.org, website: www.worldbank. org/financialcrisis, www.worldbank.org/gender

The financial crisis section of the World Bank's website brings together information on the Bank's work on the crisis, including links to research reports, news releases, and blogs, although at the time of this journal going to press, there appeared to be very little, if any, content focusing on gender and the crisis. The Bank's work on gender appears on the 'Gender and development' area of the website and includes a description of The World Bank Group's four-year Gender Action Plan; although, once again, there seemed to be, at the time of going to press, scarcely anything relating to gender and the crisis.

Index

Note: page numbers in **bold** refer to figures and tables.

mothers
  responsibility for children 45
  single 18, 22, 81
Muslims 90–1

neoliberalism 45
Netherlands 21
New Financial Architecture 116, 125
NGOs (non-government
  organization) 1, 10–11, 52, 80

ODI (Overseas Development
  Institute) 31n4, 132, 134
Overseas Filipino Workers (OFWs) 76

Pakistan 108
PEAs, *see* private employment
  agencies
Peru 6, 79–84, 136
Philippines
  and Asian financial crisis 67–8
  migrant domestic workers from
    89, 96
  poverty in 70–4
  recommendations for 75–7
  stimulus packages in 137
  women's employment in 7, 67, 69
Philippines' Overseas Employment
  Administration Agency (POEA) 97
Portugal 20
poverty
  coping strategies for 2, 72, 107,
    134–5
  feminization of 70, 81, 83–4
  and global economic crisis 1
  transient 73
poverty-alleviation programmes 10
private employment agencies (PEAs)
  90, 93, 95–6, 98
productive economy 6, 10
productivity, agricultural 25, 30, 138
productivity growth 16, 23, 28
prostitution, *see* sex work
public employment programmes 45

public sector
  budget cuts in 18–19, 22, 45
  revenues 18
  spending 19, 25, 31
public works programmes 138–9

remittances
  drops in 18–19, 79, 96, 129, 132
  effects of loss 22
  to Ethiopia 87–8, 92, **94**, 95
rentiers 17
reproductive economy
  definition of 4–5
  impact of crisis on 8, 43–5

SAPs (Structural Adjustment
  Programmes) 2, 4, 25, 75
Saudi Arabia 88–9, 91, 93, 96
saving rates 26
school feeding programmes 23, 137,
  139
self-employment 21, 111n1, 116
SEWA (Self-Employed Women's
  Association) 106
sex work 6, 53, 82, 93
sexual abuse 92
sexual harassment 7, 55, 81–2
social assistance 137
social capital 90
social compact 89, 95
social equity 137
social infrastructure 23, 25, 27, 30,
  43
social insurance 72, 76, 137
social networks 90, 136
social protection 3, 44, 76, 84,
  101–2, 111, 130, 136–40
social safety nets 3, 7, 9, 21, 24–5,
  27, 44–5, 62, 110, 129, 140
social services
  basic 10
  private sector provision of 4
  state funding of 9, 19, 129
social welfare 137, 139

South Africa
  child support in 139, 141n7
  informal economy in 7
  street trading in 117–25, **117,
    120–3**
  volunteer work in 46
South Korea 20, 26, 42–4, 135, 137
Spain 20
stimulus packages, *see* fiscal
  stimulus
street traders 8, 102–5, 115, 117,
  119, 124
Structural Adjustment Programmes
  (SAPs) 2, 4, 25, 75
sub-prime lending 17, 31n1

Thailand
  and Asian financial crisis 67
  economic corridors in 54–5
  effects of economic crisis on 52,
    56–8
  health services in 135
  migrant workers in 7, 51–62
  women's employment in 6, 19
  working conditions in 55, 59
tourism 18–19, 90
training programmes 24, 76

Uganda 2, 22
undocumented workers 97
unemployment
  differing effects of 134
  in Gulf countries 93
  increases in 18, 117
  policy reponses to 17–18
  in South Africa 116–18, 123, 125n2
unemployment insurance 21, 24, 43
UNICEF (United Nations Children's
  Fund) 132
unions 42, 55, 62, 84
United States, inequality in **16**
unpaid work
  gender balance of 44
  importance of 1

in reproduction sector 4–5, 39–40;
  see also women, unpaid care
  work of
urbanization 131

violence 6, 11, 80, 134–5
volunteer work 4, 40, 44, 46

wages
  fall in real 16–17
  minimum 7, 30, 45, 56, 76
Washington Consensus 4, 12n2
waste-pickers 8, 103–4, 108, 110,
  112n6
women
  and capital mobility 17
  and credit 29, 41–2
  and decision-making 38, 41
  earnings of 6, 9–10, 80, 107
  enterprises of 29, 41
  family responsibilities of 75,
    107–8, 123–4, 131, 134–5
  as farmers 25, 31
  in informal economy 104
  and microfinance 5
  as migrant workers 8, 51, 53–4,
    56–7, 61–3, 92, 95, 97–8
  in official bodies 24
  organizations of 11
  and poverty 83
  precariousness of employment 19,
    80, 105
  right to employment 20
  and service cuts 3
  and social protection 138–9
  as street traders 105, 115, 119–24
  supporting employment of 140
  trafficking of 6
  unemployment of 19, 21, 61, 68,
    70, 79, 82, 134
  unpaid care work of 8, 30, 40,
    131
  unpaid work of 44
  violence against 80, 134–5

The *Working in Gender and Development* series brings together themed selections of the best articles from the journal *Gender & Development* and other Oxfam publications for development practitioners and policy makers, students, and academics. Titles in the series present the theory and practice of gender-oriented development in a way that records experience, describes good practice, and shares information about resources. Books in the series will contribute to and review current thinking on the gender dimensions of particular development and relief issues.

Other titles in the series include:
Gender-Based Violence
HIV and AIDS
Climate Change and Gender Justice